Greece & Rome

NEW SURVEYS IN THE CLASSICS No. 26

HOMER

BY

R. B. RUTHERFORD

Published for the Classical Association

OXFORD UNIVERSITY PRESS

1996

Oxford University Press, Walton Street, Oxford OX2 6DP

Oxford New York Toronto
Delhi Bombay Calcutta Madras Karachi
Petaling Jaya Singapore Hong Kong Tokyo
Nairobi Dar Es Salaam Cape Town
Melbourne Auckland

and associated companies in
Berlin Ibadan

ISSN 0017–3835
ISBN 019 922209–6

Printed in Great Britain
by Bell and Bain Ltd.,
Glasgow

PREFACE

J. B. Hainsworth's survey in this series, published in 1969, has proved its worth as an expert overview of the many problems arising from the research of Milman Parry and his followers in the field of oral poetry. It remains an acute and wide-ranging exposition, but the passage of almost thirty years has inevitably meant that parts of it now look dated; nor have Hainsworth's own views remained static.[1] A re-issue in 1979 included a useful bibliographical appendix, but scholarly output has enormously increased since then, and with the expansion in scale of the New Surveys series, the editorial board felt that Homer merited a completely new treatment in this larger format. It would be discourteous if I failed to stress that I do not see my own essay as 'superseding' Hainsworth's: each of us is expressing his own views and writing from his own perspective, in the hope that a synthesizing account may be helpful to students and colleagues. If bibliography is more prominent in my own survey, that is partly because of the increased space available; nevertheless, the body of the text presents not an orthodoxy but a personal view, naturally selective and (in such a controversial field) inevitably vulnerable to criticism.

The ideal interpreter of Homer would have an expert knowledge of Mycenaean archaeology, Mediterranean geography, Indo-European philology and oral traditions in many different languages, as well as of every aspect of archaic Greek culture, from the cults of Apollo to the minutiae of dialect change. I cannot claim to be such a paragon, and some ignorance is perhaps an advantage when space is at a premium. The emphasis in the following pages is on the poems themselves: origins, transmission and reception receive some attention, but for the most part I have assumed that the reader is interested in the *Iliad* and the *Odyssey* as narrative poetry and in ways of reading and appreciating those texts. Inevitably, I have sometimes had to deal with questions that I have discussed elsewhere, in various articles and particularly in my commentary on *Odyssey* xix and xx. I have, however, tried to vary the examples and keep duplication to a minimum. The *Odyssey* has been given rather less attention than the *Iliad*, partly because of the existence of these other contributions.

It was obvious from the start that the bibliography could not possibly include everything relevant. I am very much aware that I have had to omit many deserving and interesting books and articles, but I feel sure that colleagues will recognize the impossibility of the task, and hope that non-specialists will still be able to find enough guidance in a vast field.

Translations of ancient texts are my own unless otherwise stated. When I have adopted those of others, I have taken the liberty of imposing uniformity in the matter of proper names, feeling that it would be too confusing to find forms such as 'Ajax' in my own text alongside 'Aias' in the quotations.

I am extremely grateful to three colleagues who generously gave up precious time during September 1995 to read the entire survey in draft at distressingly short notice: Simon Hornblower, Robert Parker, and Peter Parsons. Their comments and criticisms were invaluable to me, but they must not be held responsible for any errors or intransigence of mine. Finally, it is a pleasure to thank Ian McAuslan for his calm and efficient help as editor. His prompt attention to my queries and careful inspection of draft material made my task a great deal easier, and it is flattering to have been invited to contribute to a series which has always been important and has achieved new distinction in recent years.

R. B. Rutherford

NOTE

1. Note esp. his contributions to the Cambridge *Iliad* and Oxford *Odyssey* projects; also Hainsworth, *The Idea of Epic* (Berkeley, Los Angeles and London, 1991); 'Ancient Greek [sc. Heroic Poetry]', in Hatto 1980, 20–47; 'The complexity of theme and emotion in the *Iliad*', in *La Epica Griega y su influencia en la literatura espanola (aspectos literarios, sociales y educativos)*, ed. J. A. López Férez (Madrid, 1994), 25–38.

CONTENTS

NOTES ON CITATIONS AND ABBREVIATIONS

For brevity, I cite books of the *Iliad* by Arabic numerals (1–24), those of the *Odyssey* by lower-case Roman (i–xxiv). Thus 'see 12. 35' is a reference to the thirty-fifth line of book 12 of the *Iliad*, 'xii. 35' a reference to the equivalent line in the *Odyssey*. As for bibliography, major works which are mentioned throughout are listed at the end of the survey and cited by the 'Harvard system' (e.g. 'Kirk 1962'); details of books and articles mentioned only in one connection, or tangentially relevant, are given in full in the notes. This compromise is not ideal, but on the whole it does save space.

Most of the abbreviations of ancient authors or modern periodicals follow familiar conventions, and can be interpreted from (e.g.) the list in the *Oxford Classical Dictionary*. The following may be less obvious:

ANET	*Ancient Near Eastern Texts relating to the Old Testament*, ed. J. B. Pritchard (3rd edn. with supplement, Princeton, 1969).
CAH	*Cambridge Ancient History*
IG	*Inscriptiones Graecae*
PMG	*Poetae Melici Graeci*, ed. D. L. Page (Oxford, 1962)
SLG	*Supplementum Lyricis Graecis*, ed. D. L. Page (Oxford, 1974)

ACKNOWLEDGEMENTS

The author and editors are grateful to Carcanet Press for permission to quote Patrick Kavanagh's poem 'Epic' from *The Collected Poems of Patrick Kavanagh* (Carcanet, Manchester, 1992); to the University of Chicago Press, for permission to quote extracts from Richmond Lattimore's translation of *The Iliad of Homer* (University of Chicago Press, Chicago, Illinois, 1951); to Oxford University Press, for permission to quote extracts from *Homer, Odyssey*, translated by Walter Shewring (Oxford, Clarendon Press, 1980); to Penguin Books Ltd., for permission to quote extracts from *Homer, The Iliad, a New Prose Translation*, by Martin Hammond (Penguin Classics, Harmondsworth, 1987); and to Penguin Books USA Inc., for permission to quote from *Homer, The Iliad*, translated by Robert Fagles (Viking Penguin, New York, 1989).

I. INTRODUCTION: BACKGROUND AND PROBLEMS

History, myth, poetry

EPIC

I have lived in important places, times
When great events were decided, who owned
That half a rood of rock, a no-man's land
Surrounded by our pitchfork-armed claims.
I heard the Duffys shouting 'Damn your soul'
And old McCabe stripped to the waist, seen
Step the plot defying blue cast-steel—
'Here is the march along these iron stones'
That was the year of the Munich bother. Which
Was more important? I inclined
To lose my faith in Ballyrush and Gortin
Till Homer's ghost came whispering to my mind
He said: I made the *Iliad* from such
A local row. Gods make their own importance.
                                        (Patrick Kavanagh)

Kavanagh's short poem confronts the reader with a number of questions
which will preoccupy us in this survey. The Homeric poems show us a
world which in many respects seems primitive and remote; even if the
expedition of the Greeks against Troy really happened, even if it took place
on the scale which the *Iliad* asserts, and lasted the full ten-year span, it
would still be 'a local row' compared with later historical conflicts, ancient
or modern. Can the bad-tempered disputes of warrior chiefs, the violent
revenge of a savage and undisciplined soldier, the lies and posturing of a
vagabond rogue, still move or excite an audience today? It will be necessary
to show here some of the ways in which Homer gives the conflict at Troy,
and the homecoming of Odysseus, a timeless importance, so that these
mere episodes in the vanished heroic age – long past even for himself and
his audience – become microcosmic images of human life. The vast subject
of Homer's influence upon later western literature cannot be even super-
ficially addressed here, but occasional comparisons and illustrations may
help to show how much subsequent poets and artists have found in the
Iliad and the *Odyssey* to enlighten and inspire their own work.

'I made the *Iliad* from such/ a local row.' But what was the local row
about, and where and when did it happen? The Greeks always assumed
that the war was an authentic historical event, and modern faith in this was

strengthened by the landmark excavations in mainland Greece and at Troy by the archaeologist Schliemann and his many successors. On the one hand, a glorious civilization had existed in Greece in times far earlier than the classical age; on the other, a city with mighty walls had existed near the Hellespont, had been rebuilt many times, and at some stage had been destroyed by fire. Supporting evidence seemed for a while to appear in Hittite documents, which mentioned a people called the Ahhijawa, a name which could be an earlier or foreign form of 'Achaeans'; and there were other possible correspondences. It was tempting to suppose that the legends were substantially true, that a great force of Greek invaders attacked and sacked the city now called 'Troy VIIA', and that some time later the fall of the Mycenaean civilization brought an end to this prosperous era; later mythology saw this in terms of an age of heroes followed by subsequent decline. The discovery that 'Linear B', the language of the Mycenaean age, was in fact an earlier form of Greek, made it possible to hypothesize a continuous tradition of poetic narrative, which preserved a record of these great days through the Dark Ages.[1]

Bold and imaginative reconstruction has on the whole been succeeded by greater caution;[2] many experts now doubt the links between the Hittite documents and the Greek legends, and even if there was a continuous tradition from Mycenaean times, we cannot assume that the tradition was free of distortion or misunderstanding (for instance, those who do not dismiss the Wooden Horse as pure fiction sometimes suppose it to be a confused echo of an Oriental siege-engine). Some features of the tradition are in any case implausible: the thousand ships, the ten years spent far from home, are surely epic exaggeration; nor can even the most romantic of readers suppress doubts about a national campaign fought to recover one leader's wife. Overseas raids and adventures are a familiar part of the epic repertoire and probably of the real-life background, as numerous passages in the *Odyssey* suggest. In the *Iliad*, Nestor recounts his own exploits as a young man in a cattle-raiding expedition against the people of Elis (11. 670–762): as has often been suggested, this may well give a more accurate idea of the scale of warfare in early Greece than the vast assemblage of peoples listed in the Catalogue of Ships.[3] At all events, even if some general account, including names, survived from Mycenaean times, it is hardly likely that any details of the course of events were preserved.

Whatever the historical facts behind the *Iliad*, they are separated from the epic itself by a gap of at least four hundred years (the traditional date for the fall of Troy was 1183 B.C., and some archaeologists place the destruction of Troy VIIA a good eighty years earlier).[4] The *Odyssey*, being a

tale about an individual's fortunes and an island community of little prominence in Mediterranean history, is still less likely to preserve much in the
way of historical reality. A great deal of the *Odyssey*, in any case, is set in a
world of magic and monsters, remote from authentic history or geography.
The poems do contain elements of an older tradition: the wealth of Agamemnon, lord of Mycenae 'rich in gold', Ajax's tower-like shield, Odysseus'
boar-tusk helmet are examples. Sometimes these memories are blurred or
conflated with later conventions: for the most part the warriors carry two
thrusting-spears, but the single heavy spear, a Mycenaean weapon, is occasionally recalled, in some passages to arouse awe and a sense of latent
power (see 16. 140 ff.). Certain verbal phrases and formulae also clearly
have a long history, and it has been argued that many of these go back to
Mycenaean times or even beyond: this would imply a long and continuous
tradition of poetry on heroic themes.[5]

Later ancient criticism assumed that the Greek epics preserved historical tradition, but it was always recognized that the poet had enhanced
or embroidered what he inherited. Herodotus remarked that Homer in the
story of the abduction of Helen had selected from various versions one
which seemed more appropriate to epic story-telling (2. 116.1, referring to
the *Cypria*), and Thucydides commented that it was natural for a poet to
exaggerate the importance of the events he described (1.10). Much has
been made of the distinctions between different types of story, such as
'saga', which is conceived as more realistic, though concerned with heroic
combat, and 'folk-tale', an elusive term often applied to more fantastic or
magical narratives; definitions are difficult, and the relation of both terms
to 'myth' is unclear.[6] In general it would seem that both Homeric poems
include folk-tale or magical elements, but the *Iliad*, with its military theme
and firm geographical setting, is more like saga, the *Odyssey*, especially in
its first half, closer to folk-tale.[7] But the contrast swiftly breaks down on
closer analysis: the *Iliad* includes a cap of invisibility, a talking horse, a
warrior who fights with a river god, and a body magically preserved against
decay; the *Odyssey*, in its own way, shows us more of social and domestic
'realities' than the more sombre and dignified *Iliad* will admit. Moreover,
the presence of the Olympian gods in both poems, but more prominently in
the *Iliad*, makes Homer a peculiarly special case: these colourful and
potent figures, intervening freely in mortal affairs for good or ill, seem to
belong to neither saga nor folk-tale, but transcend such categories.

Comparative studies have shown that even when narrative poetry of a
heroic type deals with events closer in time than the Trojan war, and better
documented, startling distortions may be introduced.[8] The *Song of Roland*

recounts an episode in the campaigns of Charlemagne, and a Latin chronicler records the death of 'Hruodlandus' in battle in 778; but the battle in
question, an attack by Basques, was of no historical importance. In the heroic style, the poet turns it into a huge conflict between Christian and
Infidel, and Roland is slain by a mighty Saracen; the whole poem embodies
the spirit of the twelfth-century Crusades.[9] Similar transformations and
intermingling of history and imagination can be found in other traditions:
the *Nibelungenlied*, for example, or the Serbian epics.[10] The Norse Saga of
the Volsungs moves from pure myth, the tale of Sigurd the Dragon-slayer,
rich in magic and close to the world of the Norse gods, into a more historical era, with Atli (Attila the Hun) in conflict with the Burgundian Gunnar
(Gundaharius); but even here the saga is demonstrably remote from
history, and combines characters who could never have met. Obviously, the
fact that modern historians can identify errors does not prove that historical accuracy is impossible in heroic epic. It has been suggested that the
broader background may often be more accurate (though less precisely
described) than the central incidents,[11] but the probable limitations of this
kind of evidence need to be recognized. It may be that the Homeric epics
tell us more about the attitudes and outlook of the Ionians of the eighth or
seventh centuries B.C. than about the actions of the Mycenaeans of the
twelfth.

The bards of Homer's age and earlier were concerned to preserve the
klea andrōn, the 'glorious deeds of men'; it would seem that they believed
these men to have existed in time long past, but recognized that they could
not guarantee every detail of their accounts. Homer invokes the Muses in
terms which admit his dependence on tradition and inspiration: 'you are
goddesses, you are present, you know all; we only hear the glorious tale,
and have no knowledge' (2. 485–6). We may doubt whether Homer had
authority in earlier poetry for every warrior he names in the *Iliad*; names
came into his mind, and seemed to fit – a sign that the Muses were at his
side, smiling upon his work. The borderline between adaptation of tradition
and creative development, here as elsewhere, is impossible for us to draw,
and may have been as hard for the original bard. The poet, then, is not
primarily a chronicler. Nor does he attempt to connect the tale he tells with
the present day, whether by offering certain characters as exemplary
figures for his own age, or more explicitly by tracing the genealogy of royal
families or particular patrons back to the heroes of old – a practice easily
paralleled in other poetic traditions, and most influentially followed by
Virgil in the *Aeneid*. Genealogy is important in the *Iliad* (less so in the more
individualist *Odyssey*, where the hero is not competing among equals), but

principally in self-assertive speeches, in which the heroes can declare themselves and define their status. There is little hint that Homer's audiences found special satisfaction in the exploits of their supposed ancestors. Even the most plausible case, the reference to the future destiny of Aeneas' descendants (picked up and developed by Roman readers), although it has been read as addressed to self-styled Aeneadae in the Troad, need not imply this.[12] The Hesiodic Catalogues illustrate a widespread interest in mythical genealogy, but firm evidence that families traced their ancestry back to mythical heroes comes from a later period, when the heroic epics are already assuming canonical status.[13] For Homer and his predecessors, the glorious past matters more than reflected glory in the present.

The Homeric poems survive complete; of other early epic poetry (as opposed to the rather different work of Hesiod) we know less than we would like, though the summaries and fragments of the so-called 'Epic Cycle' are precious evidence, probably of a somewhat later date. A major issue is whether the Homeric epics are representative or exceptional. The question can also be posed in chronological terms: do they represent the mature and typical form of the epic tradition, or a glorious final flowering? It is at any rate clear that the *Iliad* and the *Odyssey* presuppose, and were preceded by, other poems on a wide range of epic themes. This is evident from references within the poems themselves. We may distinguish references to other episodes in the Trojan war and its aftermath – the abduction of Helen, the wound of Philoctetes, the gathering at Aulis, the first embassy to the Trojans, the death of Achilles, the suicide of Ajax, and so forth – from allusions to other heroic tales which are less closely related to the Trojan war: amongst these are the story of Bellerophon, the wrath of Meleager, the war of the Seven against Thebes, the birth of Heracles and his many labours in service to Eurystheus, and the Argonautic expedition.[14] Within the Trojan saga, it is assumed that the audience knows what the situation is, why the armies are at war (see esp. 1. 159), and who the characters are: thus Achilles storms away in anger 'with Menoitius' son and his comrades' (1. 307), that is, with Patroclus, who is mentioned shortly afterwards without the identification being made explicit.

In a different category come stories about the gods. Again, it is obvious that the Olympians are familiar to the poet's audience, and that this familiarity derives not only from cult worship and visual representations but from previous song. The poems present the divine order as well-established, with a clear hierarchy of power and division of provinces (1. 533 ff., 581; 15. 185–217); we see not only from Hesiod's *Theogony* but also from a number of brief allusions in the poems that this was not an eternally fixed condition. There had been wars among the gods in earlier times: the overthrow of Cronos and the destruction of rival powers such as the Titans and Typhon are mentioned, but only in passing: the emphasis is on the security of Zeus' reign. The permanence of the gods in the *Iliad* ('happy and existing forever', 24. 99) provides the essential foil to the short-lived and suffering mortals. Elsewhere, in the references to Zeus' adulteries and the complaints of Calypso, we catch hints of a freer intermingling of gods and mortals, with regular amatory encounters involving even the king of the gods. Again the Homeric epics are selective: of the major figures only Achilles is son of a divinity, and that privilege brings him little advantage: son of a goddess and a mortal, he stands between the two worlds, not wholly belonging to either.

Homer not only cited or alluded to other poems and stories, but adapted them to play a part in his own work: for instance, a tale such as the death of Agamemnon, repeatedly cited but never retold at length in the *Odyssey*, is not evoked merely for the sake of digression, or even to advertise the range of the poet's repertoire; it is there to provide a contrast with the central story of Odysseus.[15] Other passages, such as the references to Heracles' experiences in the *Iliad*, can also be ingeniously brought into relation to the larger themes of the poem. Occasionally we may surmise that unusual or obscure versions are the inventions of the poet, to suit the argument of a particular speaker (e.g. 1. 396–406).[16] Moreover, we can see that the epics make use of a number of themes which might be used elsewhere with other heroes: heroic wrath, the wanderer's return, the descent to the underworld, the forging of divine armour, are all paralleled elsewhere in the Greek tradition, though in some cases the other texts may be echoing Homer. One case in which the borrower seems clearly to be Homer concerns the wanderings of Odysseus, and particularly the perils of the Clashing Rocks. In xii. 69–70, Circe warns the hero that only one ship has ever passed through these Rocks safely, 'the *Argo*, known to all men, sailing back from Aeetes' (70) –known, presumably, through poetry. There is good reason to think that other characters and events in these books of the *Odyssey* have also been taken over from the Argonautic saga: Circe herself, sister of Aeetes and Medea's aunt, seems to belong to that world.[17] None of this deprives Homer of originality; rather, it shows him as an active participant in a tradition which thrives on competition and constant reworking of well-established themes.

The complexity of Homer's relation to his 'sources' may be illustrated in more detail from the story of Meleager, as told by Phoenix to Achilles in book 9 of the *Iliad*.[18] Phoenix comments that until now, no-one could have found fault with Achilles' anger at Agamemnon, but if he still holds out in his refusal to accept the compensation, he may suffer the fate of Meleager, who persisted too long in a similar resentful resignation from war, and lost all chance of gifts in the end. The narrative of Meleager includes a number of parallels with the sequence of events in the *Iliad* itself: in particular, the name of the hero's wife, who eventually persuades him to abandon his wrath, is given as Kleopatra (though reference is also made to another name), apparently an anticipation of the parallel role of Patroclus, who will succeed in persuading Achilles to relent.[19] The motif of Meleager's anger, which is not found in other versions of the tale, appears to be Homer's invention, in order to bring the story into line with the main plot of the epic. A further point is that in later versions, Meleager dies on the battlefield as a result of his mother's magical revenge for the slaying of her brothers: it is disputed whether Homer suppresses this finale (which would be ill-suited to Phoenix's persuasive task), or whether the magic is a later addition to the story.[20] It is in any case clear that Phoenix's narrative performs several functions: like other 'paradigms', it offers an argument to show why the listener, here Achilles, should follow the speaker's advice. But Phoenix's perspective is limited, in several respects. He assumes that the worst thing that can happen is for Achilles to lose the chance of the gifts now being offered. In fact, in book 19, Achilles will receive the gifts anyway, despite his persistence in anger, but they will be meaningless to him because of the far greater anger and grief aroused by the death of Patroclus. In the more theological passage which precedes the Meleager-tale, Phoenix advises Achilles to respect the spirits of Prayer, the Litai, or he may suffer the consequences (502–14). This simple moralizing has sometimes been taken as endorsed by the poet,[21] but this seems to give undue importance to the words of a minor character; nor does Phoenix's ideal picture of divine justice receive much confirmation elsewhere in the poem. If Achilles is 'punished' for excess, it is in a more subtle and less overtly moralizing way. Finally, if the poet is indeed aware of some version in which Meleager's wrath ends in death, it is natural that Phoenix should suppress so grim a conclusion, but it is possible that the audience, alert to the omission, may anticipate the analogous fate of Achilles and relish the irony of the characters' efforts to evade the consequences of this parallel.[22]

The origins of Greek epic may lie further back, and further east, than dark-age Ionia. Near Eastern texts, not least the famous 'Epic of Gilgamesh', yield remarkable parallels or precedents for Homeric conceptions, episodes, and even phraseology.[23] The cosmogony implied in the account of

Oceanus and Tethys (14. 201, 302) recalls the Babylonian *Enuma elis*, the epic of creation (*ANET* 61). The conception of the gods as gathered in assembly is frequent in Akkadian and Hittite poetry. The idea of the fatal letter found in the Bellerophon-story is first attested in the story of David and Uriah (*Iliad* 6. 168–70, II Samuel 11); the Old Testament also offers a parallel to the failed seduction and revenge of Sthenoboiia (*Iliad* 6. 160–66; cf. Potiphar's wife, Genesis 39). Even the supremely Homeric statement of the opposition between god and man has precedent in the heroic realism of Gilgamesh: 'The gods, with Shamash [the sun god], they sit forever; as for mankind, numbered are their days. But you here, you fear death? . . . I will go ahead of you . . . If I myself were to fall, let me still set up my name.' (*ANET* 79).[24] Above all, Gilgamesh loses his beloved comrade Enkidu, and grieves for him with Achillean devotion, raging 'like a lioness deprived of her whelps' (*ANET* 88).[25] It has long been recognized that prominent features of Hesiod's theology (especially the myth of succession among the gods, and the sequence of ages of men) are indebted to eastern myth;[26] similarly, the Homeric poems must be set against a wider background, and recent scholarship has charted some of the channels of communication – migrant craftsmen, diviners, healers, and not least wandering bards. Oral tradition is as vital in the genesis of Greek epic as in its transmission.[27]

Rather different questions of influence and development arise with the stories which, like the Cyclops-tale, are found frequently in other cultures but only in texts of a later date than Homer: do they all depend ultimately on the story as told in the *Odyssey*, do they emerge independently, or are Homer and some or all of the later versions dependent on a common source?[28] It can at least be said that Homer did not invent the Cyclopes, who are mentioned elsewhere in the *Odyssey* in more incidental contexts; moreover, he fails to make explicit the chief feature of these monsters, and one which is crucial to the plot: that a Cyclops has only one eye (Hes. *Th.* 143).[29] There are other ways in which the story seems to have been modified or adjusted to increase tension or to suit the ethos of the *Odyssey*. Here and elsewhere, the comparison with other versions, whether older or younger than Homer, serves to bring out the particular qualities and thematic concerns of the Homeric epics.[30] Whether the perennial fascination of these themes depends on their intrinsic merits as material for exciting stories or on some deeper psychological or anthropological roots is a question which goes beyond the province of the literary critic.[31]

Composition and Transmission

The origins and early context of the Homeric epics are scarcely recoverable even in outline; what follows can only be a sketch of the endlessly fascinating, yet seemingly insoluble, problems embraced by the 'Homeric question'.

We do not know who Homer was, and ancient biographies, largely fanciful in the manner of the genre, are no help; the fact that there was even speculation as to the origin of the name proves that antiquity was no wiser than we are about the man behind it.[32] Although the so-called 'separatists' had their doubts,[33] most people assumed that the same man composed the *Iliad* and the *Odyssey*, and it remains convenient to use the name 'Homer' as shorthand for the creator of both epics, even if one supposes that the *Odyssey* is in fact by a later imitator. Equal darkness covers the place and date of composition of the epics. Notoriously, different cities and islands of the eastern Mediterranean competed for the honour of being Homer's birthplace (this dispute is the subject of various epigrams in *Anth. Pal.* 16. 293–99). The Ionian coastline, or the island of Chios with its later association with 'Homeridae' ('sons of Homer'), have strong claims; by the time of Simonides (early fifth century B.C.) Homer could be cited as simply 'the Chian' (fr. 19 West[2]). Some of his descriptive passages concerning places near Troy probably rest on first-hand experience: in particular, he knows that Poseidon could have seen Troy from the topmost peak of Samothrace, though the island of Tenedos might have been thought to obstruct his view.[34] That he had similar knowledge of Odysseus' kingdom, the island of Ithaca, is less likely, given the geographical difficulties, and his acquaintance with remoter regions such as Egypt, important though these are in the *Odyssey*, was extremely limited.[35]

The question of the date of composition of the *Iliad* and *Odyssey* is bound up with the problem of the process of creation and transmission.[36] In antiquity the Homeric poems were seen as *literary* creations: that is, readers supposed that they had been created with the aid of writing, as was the work of later poets. Although the Jew Josephus declared that Homer was illiterate, this was for no good critical reason, but formed part of a polemic in which he denigrated the classic texts of paganism in contrast with the authority and dignity of the scriptures (*Against Apion* 1. 12). In modern times it was F. A. Wolf in his *Prolegomena* (1795)[37] who set forth the fundamental objections to the hypothesis that Homer wrote his poems down himself, in the way in which we normally imagine a poet at work. The arguments partly concerned the history of writing in early Greece –

how early was the art available, and how readily would the necessary materials come to hand? – and partly exploited the inconsistencies of language, style, and construction which Wolf and his successors believed that they could detect in both epics. Hence arose the long-standing conflict between the 'analysts', those who cut up or separated the poems into layers or independent lays, and the 'unitarians', those critics who opposed this procedure and insisted on the fundamental unity and quality of both epics.[38]

The Homeric poems themselves portray heroes singing, and poets performing at feasts: Phemius at the court of Odysseus, Demodocus in the land of the Phaeacians. These bards seem not to need written texts: they perform with instrument in hand, a *kitharis* or a *phorminx*, conventionally translated 'lyre', and are probably imagined as chanting rather than singing throughout. They follow the directions of their aristocratic patrons: Penelope asks Phemius to choose another song, and the disguised Odysseus calls for a laudatory narrative of his own exploits in the sack of Troy. Telemachus mentions the attraction of a new song, and Demodocus is described as singing 'the lay whose renown reached as far as broad heaven at that time' (i. 352; viii. 74). Fluency and sound organization are admired, in poetry as in rhetoric (viii. 489; ctr. 2. 213, 246); there is still higher praise for the vividness of the narrative. Odysseus tells Demodocus that he has given a marvellous account of the sufferings of the Achaeans at Troy, 'as though you yourself had been present, or heard it from another' (viii. 491). Poetry gives delight and enchants: the audience sit spellbound (i. 325–6; xvii. 518–20). It can also arouse grief and pain, particularly when it recalls to mind past suffering (i. 337–42, viii. 521–31); at the same time, the listener should be strong enough to endure this sadness and reflect on the meaning of that suffering (i. 353–5). The scenes involving bards and song can be combined to yield a coherent and subtle conception of poetry and its function.[39] These representations of singers at work, honoured in their society and rewarded with a good cut of meat, may well bear some similarity to the situation of Homer himself. Ancient readers already made this assumption, suggesting that the blind Demodocus was a mirror-image of Homer.[40] Without embracing the biographical approach, modern scholars naturally scrutinize these scenes in the hope of recovering some picture of the poet's original setting. By combining the slender indications of the poems with later Greek texts on music, imaginative scholarship has even offered a reconstruction of the original 'tune' with which the poet accompanied his song.[41]

All of this may be justifiable, but we should remember that Homer's bards are performing in a heroic world, and that the *Odyssey* in particular seems deliberately to elevate the status of the poet (e.g. xxii. 344–9, cf. xvii. 383–5). These are idealized images of the poet and his audience, particularly the picture of Demodocus in the fairyland world of Scheria. We should not draw too close a connection between the poet himself and the singers in his poem. To take only the most prominent difference, the songs of the bards in the *Odyssey* are very short; Demodocus sings three in the course of a crowded day and still leaves plenty of time for Odysseus' own tale. By contrast, it is hard, perhaps impossible, to find an occasion on which the *Iliad* or the *Odyssey* could have been actually performed: even in an age which was accustomed to long poetic recitations and appreciated the singer's art, how could such lengthy works ever be heard in their complete form? A major festival event, perhaps the Panionia at Mt. Mycale near Ephesus, could have provided a suitably grand occasion,[42] but even this context hardly explains the sheer size of the epics.

Although the concept of oral composition was already current from the time of Wolf,[43] it was the work of Milman Parry which gave this conception a central place in the interpretation and study of Homer.[44] He addressed the question of what made Homer's poems so different from later epic, and his answer was that these poems were not simply the creations of an individual, but the poems of a people, in that they were oral creations, drawing on a poetic tradition which went back over several lifetimes, even centuries. The proof of this was above all linguistic, and Parry's most important work focused on the repetitions and variations in linguistic phrases or repeated 'formulae' which are found in the Homeric texts. 'Much-enduring godlike Odysseus' is an obvious example, tied to a particular character; another, which can be used in contexts involving many characters, is 'He, wishing them well, addressed them and declared ...' (1. 253, etc.). These recurring formulae most commonly consist of whole hexameter lines, or of half-lines beginning or ending at the 'caesura' or pause-point in mid-line. In other words, they are phrases created to ease the task of a poet composing in hexameter verse.[45] Homer has often been described as an improviser, a misleading term. On the level of metrical technique and formulaic vocabulary he does indeed work with tools which were devised to ease the process of oral composition; but the *Iliad* and the *Odyssey* could not have been produced without long preparation and premeditation. A corollary of this is that the formulae, besides being useful as building-blocks, can also have an aesthetic contribution to make: 'what is technically convenient can also be poetically effective.'[46]

The systems of formulaic phrases which Parry analysed were so numerous, and showed such economy (in the sense that superfluous or duplicated phrases were kept to a minimum) that it became impossible to suppose that this was merely one poet's linguistic repertoire, all devised for his own use: it could only have been built up gradually by generations of bards. This conclusion was confirmed by philology. The language of Homer is an artificial tongue, never spoken by a single race or state at a given period; it is an amalgam of elements from different dialects and periods. Such a linguistic mixture could not have evolved in a single poet's lifetime; the poetic language was developed by poets over a period of generations. Rather than being the first and greatest of poets, Homer was shown to have composed with a long line of predecessors behind him, all of whom had contributed to the subject matter and diction of his own work. Perhaps he was at the mid-point of this tradition, or perhaps the *Iliad* and the *Odyssey* represented its final peak. Some have rebelled against Parry's conclusions, feeling that they deny Homer any claim to originality or invention; but this is to misconceive the debate. Any artist imitates or makes use of his predecessors; the relation between tradition and innovation is a subtle and fruitful one, for the literate and for the oral poet.[47] Nevertheless, the Homeric epics, though created in a tradition, stood out even in antiquity as exceptional in quality; this was, after all, the verdict of Aristotle and of Horace.[48]

Parry's researches were published gradually rather than being brought together in a book, and his untimely death in 1935 meant that some time elapsed before his ideas had their full impact. Nor have they ever influenced continental scholarship as much as they have Anglo-American work on Homer, though there are signs that things are changing. Much has been done to extend and develop his ideas, particularly in the analysis of formulaic systems. Parry was mainly concerned with the noun-epithet formulae ('much-enduring godlike Odysseus' and the like), but made some moves towards the examination of larger sequences in terms of recurrent patterns: motifs, themes, typical scenes and so forth.[49] Subsequent work in this area, notably by Fenik, has been especially valuable.[50] By comparing a set of (e.g.) arming-scenes or scenes in which a stranger arrives and is given welcome, episodes which occur in comparable form in different parts of Homer' work, we can see some of the poet's repertoire and observe how he plays variations on a 'standard' sequence; the overall similarity highlights differences which are often significant.[51] Sometimes we may suspect that the poet is adopting a standard sequence in order to introduce a new or unexpected element, surprising his audience. In general, Parry's methods help to make us more alert to Homer's craft as a storyteller.

In the initial excitement arising from Parry's work large claims were sometimes made about the consequences for criticism: for instance, that the Homeric poems were entirely composed of formulae (a claim that can only be sustained by unacceptably expanding the concept of a formula); that Homer, composing orally and improvising, was incapable of advance preparation or subtlety of design; that oral poetry in any case did not seek the same effects as literary poetry, and could not be judged by the same criteria; that, indeed, a whole new form of 'oral poetics' is required.[52] There has also inevitably been a reaction.[53] Some of Parry's formulations were clearly vulnerable, and some of his followers went too far in ruling out any kind of traditional 'literary' analysis. On the other hand, it is evident that the formulaic style, and other features of Homeric poetry which distinguish it from the epics of Apollonius or Virgil or Milton, do need to be taken into account in criticism. At the very least, Parryism can explain the frequency with which lines or phrases are repeated in the poems. It is surely necessary to go further, and to see Homer's narratives as composed for performance.

Parry stressed the element of tradition in the Homeric epics, while others have sought to isolate particularly creative uses or modifications of traditional material, or even maintained that Homer is working against or re-moulding the tradition.[54] More specifically, the analysts had complained that Homer often used language inappropriately, for instance in applying 'stock' epithets where they did not fit (Penelope's 'fat' hand in xxi. 6 was a notorious example). Parry went so far as to claim that the poet used these phrases so automatically that they no longer possessed a real meaning for him. What needs saying here is that the cases of inept use are remarkably rare, and need to be balanced against examples of Homer's conscious and tactful adjustment of formulae to suit a particular situation. A small but telling instance occurs at 16. 298, when Zeus, who is often given the epithet 'gatherer of the clouds', is described instead as 'gatherer of the lightning', a variant which is found only here. The reason is clear: the poet is describing how Zeus disperses the clouds, and the normal epithet would naturally jar.[55] Another approach is to explore the complexity of Homer's diction and styles: whereas Parryism seemed to imply a monolithic formulaic style, recent work has made clear that there are important distinctions between the style of the speeches and that of the narrative; moreover, different speakers may be characterized by different styles.[56] In all these areas, what matters is to recognize that both tradition and originality are combined, even if there are limits to how far we can define the relationship between the two.

The other aspect of Parry's work which particularly caught the imagination of his followers was the comparative approach, pursued through fieldwork on existing oral poetic traditions, above all in Yugoslavia in the

1930s.[57] There it proved possible to hear, record and question bards composing without literacy, and to test the reliability of their memories of previous songs. Through this fieldwork, so Parry believed, a poetic tradition comparable with that of Homer could be observed and preserved. Fascinating though the comparison has proved, subsequent scholarship has been cautious in making deductions about the consequences for Homer. In quality and metrical subtlety the Yugoslav poems seem to fall short of Homer's; nor do these bards generally compose on such a large scale except on special request. The differences between ancient Ionia and modern Europe mean that special caution is needed in tracing the development or degeneration of an oral poetic tradition.[58] These analogies can only be suggestive, not probative. In the end Parry's work on modern traditions may be found less valuable for Homeric studies than his analysis of Homer's own style and formulae.

Parry tended to say or imply that his researches had 'proved' that Homer was an oral poet, in the sense of one who not only performed orally but made no use of writing in the composition of his works or at any stage. Not all critics have accepted this conclusion. It does seem clear that we are dealing with an oral *tradition* – that is, the nature of Homeric language can only be accounted for by supposing Homer to be the inheritor of a body of traditional oral poetry, and to be re-using the style and diction of his elders. This would not necessarily imply that writing played no part at all in the creation or preservation of Homer's own poetry. Lord and others have supposed that Homer himself was illiterate but dictated his works to willing disciples or scribes, so making it possible for the master's works to live on.[59] Others have wished to go a step further and cut out the middle-man: could not Homer himself have learned to write and used this opportunity to preserve, perhaps to enhance and enlarge, his greatest poem? It has been suggested that the discovery of writing itself could have been the stimulus which prompted a poet of exceptional gifts to create or develop a poem of extraordinary scope and length, in the knowledge that the instrument now existed to ensure his work's survival.[60] More far-fetched is the hypothesis that the alphabet was itself devised specifically as a means of preserving epic poetry.[61]

Current orthodoxy places the introduction of the alphabet from the Phoenician into the Greek world in the late ninth or early eighth century: the earliest known Greek inscriptions come from *c.*770–750 B.C.[62] Whether an alphabet, if available, would have been utilized to put Homer's poetry in a permanent form, or whether suitable writing materials could be obtained at this date, will partly depend on the importance which we suppose was attached to poetry in this period. Papyrus was an expensive import even in fifth-century Athens; leather has also been suggested.[63] The difficulties are formidable, but the notion that the *Iliad* was consigned to writing from the start, at a date in the late eighth or early seventh centuries, is not a physical impossibility, and may seem more attractive if we find it hard to understand the composition of so massive an epic for performance alone. The alternative is to accept an interval before the epic was committed to writing, a period in which it was preserved through memory alone, first the memory of Homer himself, then perhaps of a son or pupil.

Modern readers of Homer – 'readers' is the key word – find it almost impossible to imagine the effort of memory involved in preserving long poetic texts such as these without any aide-mémoire. True, actors and operatic singers achieve feats scarcely less miraculous even in our own time, but they have a written text to memorize. It can be argued, however, that this is the wrong model. According to Parry, and to many who have studied oral poetic traditions more widely than he, the singer is not memorizing and reproducing, but composing afresh, re-creating; each new performance is in a sense a new song, and tape-recorders will show differences of some significance even when a singer does claim to be repeating 'the same' song. According to this view, the poet is in large part 'improvising', a word with disturbing implications. Did the *Iliad*, or parts thereof, go through this process in Homer's lifetime, being re-created many times? In that case, we may well suspect that the poet refined his work and added fresh beauties, rather than simply starting afresh each time; but how can we be sure that we have the 'best' version? The problem becomes greater when a different poet takes over the song, and remakes it anew. If a period of several generations intervenes before the poem is committed to writing, it may undergo extensive changes. In a way, it is not 'Homer's' poem. We may think of the paradox of the axe hanging on the wall for generations: if the blade has been replaced twice, the handle once, is it still 'grandfather's axe'? Hence the attractions of assuming a literate Homer; a written text may be subject to the normal mishaps of miscopying, but at least imposes some fixity. Alternatively, some look hopefully to the so-called Homeridae, who, if they recognized the stature of their poet, may perhaps have sought to memorize rather than re-create.[64] The evidence is insufficient to establish a firm sequence of events; but it must be admitted that only the natural optimist will be able to suppose that the authentic words of 'Homer' have come down to us uncontaminated and undistorted.

Early influence and established status

Homer is traditionally paired with the Boeotian Hesiod, the first Greek writer to refer to himself by name (*Th.* 22). Which poet was chronologically earlier was already debated in antiquity, but it is conventional, on no very strong grounds, to put Hesiod later. Partly this is simply because we feel we know him better: in both the *Theogony* and the *Works and Days* Hesiod has things to say about himself, his poetic calling and his opinions on morality and religion; he does not maintain the epic anonymity and detachment. The arguments for Hesiod's dates hinge on his participation in the funeral games for Amphidamas, a warrior of Chalcis in Euboea, which most interpreters associate with the Lelantine war of the late eighth or early seventh centuries.[65] But whatever Hesiod's date, there is no reason to assume a close relationship between his work and Homer's; Hesiod is clearly aware of the epic tales of Thebes and Troy, and has many phrases and formulae in common with Homer, but this only means that heroic narrative and didactic or catalogue poetry are not mutually exclusive genres.[66]

Similar questions arise with the other epic poems which survived from the archaic period but later disappeared – works such as the *Cypria* and the *Sack of Ilium*. Many of these were also ascribed to Homer, though other names were current and scepticism is visible in Herodotus (2. 116 f. on the *Cypria*); the fifth-century tragedians drew on them as readily as on Homer. Fragments survive from most of these epics, but more valuable are the summaries of the poems on the Trojan war compiled by Proclus, perhaps in the 5th century A.D.[67] In fact it seems likely that most of these were later than Homer, though drawing, like him, on earlier poetry. The Trojan epics were probably composed to fill in the gaps in the narrative of the war, complementing the *Iliad* and *Odyssey* themselves; the whole series became known as the 'epic cycle'. Aristotle drew a clear distinction between the quality of the two epics which we now ascribe to Homer and that of the rest; thereafter the term 'cyclic' was attached to the other poems and acquired a pejorative sense.[68] It is of course hazardous to draw comparisons when the poems themselves do not survive, but there is some reason to think that in style and construction, as also more clearly in length, they fell short of Homer's level. At any rate, their relevance to Homer is limited, since most appear to have been composed at a later date, perhaps in the later seventh century. Finally there are the so-called 'Homeric' hymns, again misleadingly ascribed to the same master poet. Of the collection which survives many are short and late: the most important are also the longest and probably the earliest – hymns to Demeter, Aphrodite, Apollo, and Hermes. Of these the first two are influenced by the Homeric epics or closely-related poems; all four are composed in a comparable style. The chief difference between these and Homeric epic is that the gods, not mankind, are at the centre of the stage (as the hymnic form makes natural): their birth, youth, powers and characteristic activities are recounted and celebrated, in narratives which are not devoid of humour but which avoid the more whimsical treatment of the gods which we find in Homer, especially in the *Iliad*. The realities of cult action and worship in specific shrines are much more prominent: Eleusis for Demeter, Delphi and Delos for Apollo. Homer treats the gods as selectively but with greater freedom.[69]

It is consoling to enumerate a number of concrete testimonies, though as so often in this early period, they involve their own uncertainties. The Spartan poet Callinus, a figure of the seventh century, is said to have referred to Homer by name (Paus. 9.9.5) – though regarding him as author of a poem on Thebes, not of the surviving epics. Although 'echoes' of Homeric scenes and lines are often illusory, since the imitation may be of epic material in general, and not of what we think of as Homer,[70] certain adaptations of memorable scenes seem to place Homer securely in the period prior to Alcman, Alcaeus, and above all Stesichorus.[71] We may also attribute the popularity of certain scenes in art (not least the Cyclops episode) to increasing knowledge of the Homeric poem: one early representation of the Cyclops comes from around 670 B.C. (an amphora from Eleusis).[72] Other arguments aimed at dating sections of the poem are unsound[73] or more speculative, but we should attach some weight to the judgement of archaeologists that Achilles' reference to the wealth of Delphi would be improbable much before *c.*700.[74] Janko has scrutinized the language of Homer, Hesiod, and the Homeric Hymns from the standpoint of philology: applying a number of criteria of linguistic change, he finds confirmation of the 'traditional' sequence of relative dates, with *Iliad* first, then *Odyssey*, then Hesiod's *Theogony, Works and Days*, and later still the Hymns. He also believes that his findings establish, within a margin for error, secure 'absolute' datings for each work: the *Iliad* was composed between 750–25 B.C., the *Odyssey* between 743–13. If these claims are justified, the Homeric poems are more firmly anchored in chronology than ever before; and even if one doubts the absolute datings, the conclusions as to relative chronology are encouragingly close to those deduced by other criteria: Hesiod himself makes clear that the *Works and Days* is a later poem than the *Theogony*, and we shall see that there is good reason to think the *Odyssey* later than the *Iliad*. To sum up, we may reasonably see Homer as composing the *Iliad* between 750 and 700,[75] with the *Odyssey* following after a interval of at least a decade; over the next century they became gradually more widely known, and in the period from 600 onwards we may assume that they already had special status as, effectively, 'classic' texts to which other poets and artists might consciously allude.[76]

None of this is incompatible with purely oral transmission, though as we have seen there are difficulties with that theory. According to later sources it was in the sixth century, during the reign of the Athenian tyrant Pisistratus (d. 527) and his sons, that an authoritative written text of Homer was prepared, for use by rhapsodes who recited the epics at the great festival of the Panathenea.[77] These sources are not only much later but mutually contradictory, and there have been attempts to dismiss the whole 'Pisistratean recension' as a fiction; but although we should not envisage anything like a scholarly publication, it seems likely that some such centralized text was established, and that this stage in the tradition accounts for some of the 'Atticisms' or traces of Attic dialect in our texts of Homer. The idea that before this date no coherent epic songs existed, and that it was Pisistratus who brought various songs together and created 'Homer', was brilliantly asserted by Wolf and has been re-argued since,[78] but seems fundamentally implausible: the Greeks thought of Homer as an older figure, and did not associate him with Athens; the Athenians themselves make a poor showing in the *Iliad*, which makes it unlikely that the poem was radically modified in that city; the assertions that the Athenians did in fact interpolate certain passages presupposes a pre-existing text; and the theory contradicts the chronological arguments of Janko. It is much more likely that Pisistratus 'procured the first complete set of rolls to cross the Aegean' (Janko 1992, p. 37), and that his contribution was later exaggerated.

The earliest testimony to this activity by the Pisistratid family ascribes it to Hipparchus, his son (d. 514): 'he first conveyed the poems of Homer to this country, and made the rhapsodes go through them in order at the Panathenaia, taking turns at the task, as they still do today' (Pl. *Hipparchus* 229b). These rhapsodes ('weavers of song'), professional reciters of poetry which is not their own, are a new phenomenon, distinct from the genuine oral poet.[79] Plato elsewhere satirizes the pretensions of one such figure, the complacent Ion, who can perform Homer to perfection but cannot explain him. The poets and their kinsmen (Homeridae and the like) no longer have a special authority over their poetry; by becoming a classic, Homer has entered the public domain.[80]

A more specific allegation in antiquity, preserved in the Homeric scholia, was that book 10 of the *Iliad*, often called the *Doloneia*, was no part of the original poem, but was separately composed and incorporated in the epic by Pisistratus (schol T. 10.1). The association of the change with Pisistratus may be merely the result of the earlier stories about his involvement with the Homeric text, but the suggestion that book 10 is a later addition gains some support from the linguistic, structural, and ethical peculiarities of that book, as well as from the lack of cross-references to it in the rest of the *Iliad*. Although the tenth book presupposes the *Iliad*, the *Iliad* does not need the *Doloneia*.[81] This leads on to the general question of addition to and subtraction from the Homeric text during the course of its transmission. If a whole book has been interpolated, what other changes may have been made at different times? Other cases were indeed cited, or at least problems were identified, by ancient critics: most alarmingly, the conclusion of the *Odyssey* (see below, ch. 3, p. 74).[82] By comparison with these, the occasional slips where 'Homer nods'[83] seem of little significance: 'Schedios is killed by Hector not once but twice; we do not weep for him. Chromios is killed three times, and innumerable eyes are dry.'[84]

It hardly needs saying that commitment of the epics to writing, and even the possible establishment of an 'authorized' text for the Panathenaic recitations, did not ensure a calm and straightforward transmission of the text from that point to the present day. In virtually all textual traditions, the work comes down to us by various routes, and is recopied many times; even setting aside deliberate interference, it is an established fact that new errors will occur at every stage. Although there is much that we cannot reconstruct, it seems clear that Homer circulated in many versions which differed significantly from one another during the centuries after Pisistratus: the evidence comes partly from quotations in other literary sources, partly from the early papyri, which often deviate from the text that later became 'standard', in particular including additional lines. The divergences are sometimes so marked that scholars refer to early examples as the 'wild' papyri. Alexandrian scholars did much work identifying possibly spurious lines and deciding between variant readings; after the third century B.C. the text seems to settle in more or less the form which we have inherited, and it is usual to associate this development with the name of Aristarchus, one of the most distinguished scholars of Alexandria.[85]

In modern times, the analysts claimed they had identified many later additions, and sought to reduce the poem to its earliest and purest state by purging it of such intrusions. This practice is misguided and in any case fruitless: even supposing that all such cases were objectively identified, we cannot assume that they have been simply added to a core which remains uncontaminated. If that assumption is not made, then the supposed original is irrecoverable. But in an oral tradition the very concept of an 'original' version may in any case be a chimera. Nevertheless, many critics have continued to build up counter-arguments to the more drastic version of analytic criticism, showing how well-integrated and intricately structured both epics in fact are. Scenes are demonstrably connected, later events are foreshadowed, explicit anticipation is common, and the poet has a firm control over an extended but carefully organized plot. Against those who maintained that oral composition must be loose and 'paratactic', this new wave of unitarians insists on the subtlety and complexity of Homer's art. This is a version of the argument from design: random combination or cumulative addition could not have resulted in this satisfyingly ordered microcosm. Schadewaldt and Reinhardt, Bannert and Reichel in German, Macleod and Taplin in English, have charted an impressive range of connections and cross-references which surely imply the master hand of a 'monumental poet' who planned the *Iliad* as a whole. Similar arguments have been applied to the *Odyssey* by Garvie and myself among others. It remains true that some of these intricate structures are more visible and significant than others; some, it may be said, are perceptible only to the eye of faith. More disquieting is the argument of Nagy and Seaford, that many of the thematic echoes and links which the unitarians detect can equally be explained by the conscious and sensitive development of the poem by a succession of bards; to seek a single poet of surpassing genius, according to them, is merely romantic misunderstanding of the nature of an oral tradition.[86] The dialogue between the advocates of orality and literacy, imitation and innovation, tradition and individuality, becomes ever more challenging.

Reception, ancient and modern

'From the beginning following Homer, because all have learned [from him?] ...' (Xenophanes B10). 'It is they [Homer and Hesiod] who by their poetry gave the Greeks a theogony and gave the gods their titles; they who assigned to them their statuses and skills and gave an indication of their appearance.' (Hdt. 2. 53).[87] 'Consequently, Glaucon, when you encounter admirers of Homer who assert that this poet has been the educator of Greece, and that ... one should organize and lead one's whole life in accordance with this poet's work ...' (Pl. *Rep.* 10. 606e). These and many other passages attest the special prestige of Homer in the classical period. Simonides could refer to him as 'the Chian' (above), but in time he became simply 'the poet' – no ambiguity was possible. Aristophanes' Aeschylus calls him 'divine' (*Frogs* 1034); the real Aeschylus was said to have declared his tragedies 'fish-slices from the banquet of Homer' (Athen. 8. 347c). The highest praise for a later poet was to call him 'Homeric' (D. L. 4. 20, on Sophocles; 'Longinus' 13. 3). Nor was Homer the pathfinder of tragedy alone; he can also be seen as the inspiration for historiography, which shares his concern to preserve the 'glorious deeds of men', of rhetoric, even of New Comedy. Quintilian and others compared Homer with the Ocean, which encircled the world and flowed into every lesser river.[88] Homer has indeed been called 'the Bible of the Greeks', but this description requires some important qualifications. At no stage were the epics sacred texts; they were not kept in temples or interpreted by priests; although Homer was preeminent by the sixth century, other early texts were quoted and cited to illustrate mythical 'facts' or to back up an argument; as we have seen, Herodotus paired Homer with Hesiod as a formative influence on the Greeks' conception of the gods. Above all, Homer was not venerated without question. 'Poets tell many a lie', said the Athenian Solon, echoing Hesiod.[89] The Pre-Socratic thinker Xenophanes was more specific. 'Homer and Hesiod attributed to the gods all the things which bring reproach and disgrace among men – theft, adultery, deceit' (B11). Heraclitus was more forthright: 'Homer deserves to be thrown out of the public contests and given a beating' (B42). Pindar expressed reservations as to the reliability of Homer's testimony about Odysseus: 'I hold that the renown of Odysseus is more than his sufferings, because of Homer's sweet singing ... Art beguiles and cheats with its tales' (*Nem.* 7. 20–3). Plato refers in the *Republic* to 'an ancient quarrel between poetry and philosophy' (10. 607bc),[90] and excises offending passages, particularly those which show gods or heroes in an ignoble light. The controversy over the immorality of Homer's gods continued throughout antiquity.[91] But the morality of the heroes, the impetuous Achilles and the devious Odysseus, also aroused strong feelings. The tragic dramas of fifth-century Athens constantly rework Homeric themes and scrutinize epic values from the standpoint of a later age: enthusiastic admiration is mingled with questioning and even protest.[92]

Interpretation arises out of competition and polemic, for later poets sought to compete with or surpass the epic master. 'Potter contends with potter, bard with bard', said Hesiod (*WD* 26).[93] Hesiod's own reference to the Muses' lies has sometimes been taken as a jibe at epic narrative, probably wrongly. Stesichorus revised Homer's mythology and his own, rejecting the tale that Helen went to Troy with Paris (*PMG* 192). In the sixth century Theagenes allegorized Homer; in the fifth Protagoras criticized his grammar. We recognize the beginnings of scholarly commentary.[94] Many passages of Homer are quoted and discussed, not always in negative vein, by speakers in Plato's dialogues or the works of Xenophon. Although interpretation was often whimsical, selecting passages to prove a point without considering context, applying anachronistic criteria, or finding fault in order to show off, the eventual effect was to generate a rich and varied body of critical discussion.

The special importance of Homer meant that his poems, and especially the *Iliad*, were more closely studied than any other works of pagan antiquity. Historians debated the date of the fall of Troy, rhetoricians analysed the forms of argument employed in the speeches, students of mythology sought to reconcile or relate different legends, grammarians puzzled over linguistic forms, tried to explain difficult words, and assessed the merits of variant readings. One work which would have shed much light on the state of interpretation in classical times was Aristotle's *Homeric Problems*, now lost except for a few extremely suggestive fragments; the much more sketchy treatment of some Homeric topics in a chapter of the *Poetics* gives an idea of the acumen with which Aristotle must have cut through much arid or ill-conceived argument.[95] After the lengthy complaints in Plato and others about the unworthy behaviour of Homeric gods and men, there is something refreshing about the curt response of Aristotle: 'Correctness in poetry is not the same as correctness in morals, nor yet is it the same as correctness in any other art.... If an error arises through the poet's setting out to represent something incorrectly, and that is the reason why we find in the poem a mistake concerning, say, medicine or some other art, ... this does not involve the essential nature of poetry.'[96] Above all the ancient commentaries on Homer, which digest and pass on many of the observations of the great Hellenistic editors, provide not only precious mythological data and testimony to the textual tradition of the poems, but literary comment which may sometimes appear naïve, but retains interest and value.[97] It is mere arrogance to suppose that only the most recent critical methods and concepts can offer any insight to the modern reader.[98]

Many of the topics considered by scholars and students of Homer today were pioneered by the ancient critics: the study of plot-construction, characterization, rhetorical techniques, decorum and generic convention, preparation, foreshadowing, retardation, ironic double-meanings – the list could be extended. The ancients were also more alert to matters of metre and audible effects, an area much neglected in our post-oral culture.[99] Thucydides and Aristotle formulated the principle of poetic licence (Th. 1.

10.3, Arist. *Poet.* 25); Longinus in a brilliant paragraph summed up unforgettably the differences between the *Iliad* and the *Odyssey* (*On the sublime* 9. 11–15). We need not be too modest: some advances in critical understanding have become possible because we know more about philology and linguistic development than ancient scholars did, and scientific archaeology has given us a far clearer insight into the dark ages and the earlier era of Mycenae than was available to Thucydides. Other improvements are technical. We have more readable printed texts, supplemented by systematic grammars, Homeric lexica, and computerized concordances: the study of Homeric vocabulary and formulaic diction is far more straightforward for us today than it was for Aristarchus or even for Wolf and his followers.

Some modern approaches, although perhaps anticipated in earlier times in certain specific observations or insights, do seem to represent fresh steps towards a deeper understanding. One which has already been mentioned is the study of creative or imaginative development of 'stock' formulae and themes. Another is the application of a sociological or anthropological approach to Homeric society, scrutinizing the institutions, the structures of the community, and above all the values and morality which motivate the characters in the epics.[100] Closely related to this is the study of Homeric religion in relation to worship and cult in historical times: in one way this is the hardest of all tasks for modern readers, brought up in a completely different religious tradition (or in none), but there is another sense in which we have an advantage over the Greeks, since we are viewing the subject from outside, with a quite different perspective. After much groundbreaking and original research we may now hope that we have a better understanding of the relation between Homer's poetic presentation of the gods and the historical realities of ritual and cult.[101] Valuable work has been done on the use of imagery, metaphor and even symbolism (in the sense of poetic representation of physical objects which also conveys a deeper meaning), matters which at one time seemed too fanciful or sophisticated for Homer.[102] The extended simile is not the only way in which Homer adorns and obliquely sheds light on his narrative. A final example is the application of narratology – again, the systematic development of an insight already explicitly discussed in ancient texts. Narratology examines the sequence and emphases of a narrative: not just 'what happens?' but 'how is it described?'[103] It also stresses the distinction between the poet's authorial viewpoint and that of his characters, and pays special attention to the passages in which the distinction is blurred or ambiguous. Instead of taking the story for granted, we are encouraged to look more closely at the way in which it is told. This has already had beneficial effect, not least in demonstrating the futility of the old debate as to whether Homer is 'object-ive' or not; the terminology of former discussion is seen to be hopelessly over-simplified.[104] These and other critical techniques cannot be adequately explored in the abstract; they need to be illustrated through examples drawn from the epics themselves. In the pages which follow only a few instances can be provided from the abundance of Homer's store. As Dryden wrote of Chaucer, 'here is God's plenty'.

NOTES

1. The most readable discussion is that of Page 1959, a work rich in learning but now generally quoted as an example of excessive credulity. The archaeological developments are reviewed by Man-fred Korfmann, currently the doyen of the Trojan excavators, in his contribution to Latacz 1991; cf. J. Latacz, 'Neues von Troja', *Gymnasium* 95 (1988), 385–413 (Eng. version in *Berytus* 34 (1986), 97–127).

2. See esp. the collection of essays edited by Foxhall and Davies 1984; also M. J. Mellink (ed.), *Troy and the Trojan War* (Bryn Mawr, 1986), Kirk 1990, 36–50. For a penetrating essay which combines archaeological and literary finesse see E. S. Sherratt, 'Reading the Texts: archaeology and the Homeric poems' *Antiquity* 64 (1990), 807–24 = Emlyn-Jones et al. 1992, 145–65. A very different approach is adopted by D. Fehling, *Die ursprüngliche Geschichte vom Fall Trojas, oder: Interpretationen zur Troja-Geschichte* (Innsbrucker Beiträge zur Kulturwissenschaft 75, 1991), who seeks to recover the original core of the *story*, dismissing historicity.

3. On Nestor's narrative see F. Bölte, 'Ein pylisches Epos', *RhM* 83 (1934), 319–47; Hainsworth 1993, 296–8.

4. 1183 is the date accepted by Eratosthenes and Apollodorus, but many other dates were can-vassed; it is certainly hard to see how any could have been supported by proof. W. Burkert, 'Lydia between East and West or How to date the Trojan War: a study in Herodotus', in *The Ages of Homer. A Tribute to Emily Townsend Vermeule*, ed. Jane B. Carter and Sarah P. Morris (Austin, Texas, 1995), 139–48 discusses ancient dating-systems and the theories about the Trojan war, concluding that none of the dates suggested have any historical basis.

5. On the cultural amalgam see Kirk 1962, 179–92; on language, M. L. West 1988 (earlier Page 1959, ch. 6). On religion, M. P. Nilsson, *The Mycenaean Origins of Greek Mythology* (Berkeley, 1932; revised with new intr. and bibl. 1972); W. Burkert, *Greek Religion* (Oxford, 1985), ch. 1 (but p. 46 offers a warning: 'Startling correspondences with the later Greek [religious] evidence stand side by side with things totally unintelligible. Greek religion is rooted in the Minoan-Mycenaean age and yet not to be equated with it.'). On the methodological problems see Sourvinou-Inwood 1995, 18–26.

6. Rhys Carpenter 1946; Kirk 1970, 31–41, and his *The Nature of Greek Myth* (Harmondsworth, 1974); J. M. Bremmer, *Greek Religion* (*G&R* New Surveys in the Classics 24, Oxford 1994), 55–7.

7. Woodhouse 1930; Page 1973. See also Calhoun 1939.

8. J. Vansina, *Oral Tradition* (Eng. tr. 1965); id., *Oral Tradition as History* (London and Nairobi, 1985); D. P. Henige, *The Chronology of Oral Tradition: Quest for a Chimera*, (Oxford, 1974); for out-standing applications to archaic and classical Greece see R. Thomas, *Oral Tradition and Written Record in Classical Athens* (Cambridge, 1989), esp. chh. 1–2; also O. Murray, 'Herodotus and Oral History', in H. Sancisi-Weerdenburg and A. Kuhrt (ed.), *Achaemenid History II: The Greek Sources* (Leiden, 1987), 93–115.

9. Bowra 1961, 520, 530 ff.; cf. Finley et al. 1964, Hainsworth, 'The fallibility of an oral heroic tra-dition', in Foxhall-Davies 1984, 111–35, and Hainsworth 1993, 32–53. See also Taplin 1992, 26n.24.

10. Besides the items in the last note, cf. M. I. Finley, *The Use and Abuse of History* (London, 1973), ch. 1, 'Myth, memory and history'.

11. Hainsworth in Foxhall-Davies 1984, esp. 117, 121.

12. 20. 306–8; cf. *hymn to Aphrod.* 196–7; P. M. Smith, 'Aineiadai as patrons of *Iliad* XX and the Homeric Hymn to Aphrodite', *HSCP* 85 (1981), 17–58. But see Janko 1992, 19, 382, etc., arguing for disguised compliments to families claiming heroic descent.

13. On the *Catalogue of Women*, which survives only in fragments, see esp. M. L. West, *The Hesiodic Catalogue of Women* (Oxford, 1985). For early genealogies and other lists see Jeffery 1961, 59–61, S. Hornblower (ed.), *Greek Historiography* (Oxford, 1994), 9–12. On families claiming heroic ancestry see Thomas (n. 8) 100–8, 173–95.

14. 6. 155–202; 9. 527–99; 4. 370–400; 19. 95–133 (cf. 14. 249–61, etc.); xii. 69–72 (not an exhaustive list).

15. i. 29 ff., 298 ff., iii. 193 ff., 248 ff., iv. 512–37, xi. 387–434, xxiv. 20 ff., 93 ff.; A. F. Garvie, *Aeschylus: Choephori* (Oxford, 1986), ix–xii.

16. See M. M. Willcock, 'Mythological Paradeigmata in the *Iliad*', *CQ* 14 (1964), 141–51; 'Ad hoc invention in the *Iliad*', *HSCP* 81 (1977), 41–53. This position is opposed by M. Lang, 'Reverberation and mythology in the *Iliad*', in Rubino-Shelmerdine 1983, 140–64; also by Slatkin 1991, 61 ff., discussing the specific case in book 1.

17. See K. Meuli, *Odyssee und Argonautika* (Berlin, 1921), 87–115; Page 1955, 2; B. K. Braswell, *A Commentary on the Fourth Pythian Ode of Pindar* (Berlin and N.Y., 1988), 6–8.

18. For bibliography on this speech see Reichel 1994, 111n.1.

19. Kakridis 1949, 11–42; J. March, *The Creative Poet: Studies on the treatment of myths in Greek Poetry* (*BICS* Supplement 47, 1987), 27–46.

20. Bacchylides 5.94–154, Aesch. *Cho.* 594–601, Ov. *Met.* 8.260–546; Apollod. 1.8.2. J. Bremmer, 'La plasticité du mythe: Méléagre dans la poésie homérique', in C. Calame (ed.), *Métamorphoses du mythe en Grèce antique* (Geneva, 1988), 37–56 argues that this version is post-Homeric.

21. Bowra 1930, 19 23; similarly Hainsworth 1993, 56–7.

22. See further Schadewaldt 1943, 139–42, Rosner 1976, H. Bannert, 'Phoinix' Jugend und der Zorn des Meleagros', *WS* n.f. 15 (1981), 69–94; S. C. R. Swain, 'A note on *Iliad* 9. 524–99; the story of Meleager', *CQ* 38 (1988), 271–76 on the interpretation of the myth. See now Griffin's commentary, 1995, 134 ff.

23. W. Burkert, 'Oriental Myth and Literature in the *Iliad*' in T. Hägg (ed.), *The Greek Renaissance of the Eighth century BC: Tradition and Innovation* (Stockholm 1983), 51–6; 'Oriental and Greek mythology: the meeting of parallels' in J. Bremmer (ed.), *Interpretations of Greek Mythology* (London, 1988), 10–40, and Burkert 1992; cf also M. L. West 1988.

24. S. Dalley (ed. and tr.), *Myths from Mesopotamia* (Oxford, 1989), 145; Burkert, 1992, 117 f. Cf. 12. 322–8, Sarpedon's speech (quoted below, pp. 40–1).

25. M. L. West, review of the original German version (1984) of Burkert 1992, in *JHS* 106 (1986), 233–4; Dalley [see last n.], 93 (cf. *Iliad* 18. 317).

26. M. L. West, *Hesiod Theogony* (Oxford, 1966), 18–31; P. Walcot, *Hesiod and the Near East* (Cardiff, 1966); Kirk 1970, 118–31.

27. M. L. West 1988; Burkert 1992. But for a critical assessment of Burkert's approach see R. Osborne, 'À la grecque', *Journal of Mediterranean Archaeology* 6 (1993), 231–7.

28. Page 1955, ch. 1; 1973; D. Fehling, *Amor und Psyche* (Mainz, 1977), 87–100; W. Burkert, *Structure and history in Greek Mythology* (Berkeley, 1979), 156 n. 13.

29. Page 1955, 14.

30. Page 1973, Griffin 1977; cf. more generally Stanford 1963, on the evolution of the character Odysseus over the centuries.

31. Burkert (see n. 28), 30–4.

32. J. Fairweather, 'Fiction in the biographies of ancient writers', *Anc. Soc.* 5 (1974), 234–55, M. R. Lefkowitz, *The Lives of the Greek Poets* (London, 1981), 12–24; on the traditions about the poet's name and career, Allen 1924, 11–41; E. Schwartz, 'Der Name Homeros', *Hermes* 75 (1940), 1–9, and other material cited in Burkert 1987, 57 n. 1.

33. J. G. Kohl, *De Chorizontibus* (Giessen, 1917).

34. 13. 11–14, cf. Janko's n.; Kirk 1962, 273.

35. S. West 1988, 65; M. M. Austin, *Greece and Egypt in the Archaic Age*, *PCPS* Suppl. 2 (Cambridge, 1970), 11–13; Boardman 1980, ch. 4.

36. See Dodds 1968; J. L. Myres, *Homer and his Critics* (ed. D. Gray) (London, 1958); Davison in Wace-Stubbings 1962, 234–65; Hainsworth 1969, *passim*; A. Parry in M. Parry 1971, introd.; A. Heubeck, *Die homerische Frage* (Darmstadt, 1974); Clarke 1981.

37. Ed. R. Peppmüller (Halle, 1884); tr. Grafton et al., 1987. Wolf was partly anticipated by Robert Wood (1769) and others: see M. Parry 1971, x–xiv.

38. I intend to say little about the problems or objections raised by the hard-line analysts, many of

which now seem pedantic and trivial. Some cases which remain problematic are discussed in later chapters. For a pre-Parryist treatment see Bowra 1930, ch. 5; a more recent survey by Clarke 1981, ch. 4; also Page 1955, *passim*. H. van Thiel, *Ilias und Iliaden* (Basel, 1982) and *Odysseen* (Basel, 1988) documents analytic criticism exhaustively. R. D. Dawe, *The Odyssey: Translation and Analysis* (Lewes: The Book Guild, 1993) also maintains an analytic position with reference to the *Odyssey*.

39. W. Marg, *Homer über die Dichtung* (Münster 1956, 2nd edn. 1971; partly repr. in Latacz 1991b); H. Maehler, *Die Auffassung des Dichterberufs im frühen Griechentum bis zu Zeit Pindars* (Göttingen, 1963), Griffin 1980, 100–2, Macleod 1983.

40. See e.g. schol. EV viii. 63; P. Hardie, *Virgil's Aeneid: Cosmos and Imperium* (Oxford, 1986), 54f.

41. M. L. West, 'The singing of Homer and the modes of early Greek music', *JHS* 101 (1981), 113–29.

42. T. B. L. Webster, *From Mycenae to Homer* (London and New York, 1958), 267–75; Wade-Gery 1952, ch. 1; cf. Taplin 1992, 39–41.

43. M. Parry 1971, x–xxi.

44. M. Parry 1971 (Milman Parry's collected papers, with invaluable introd. by Adam Parry) remains fundamental. For clear summaries of his theories see Page 1959, 222–5; J. B. Hainsworth, *The Flexibility of the Homeric Formula* (Oxford, 1961) ch. 1.

45. For more detail on Homer's metre see M. L. West, *Greek Metre* (Oxford, 1982), 35–9, abridged as *Introduction to Greek Metre* (Oxford, 1987), 19–23. See also Hainsworth 1969, 27–8; Kirk 1985, 17–37; Rutherford 1992, 78–85. A readable essay on the subject is provided by Bowra in Wace-Stubbings 1962, 17–25.

46. Macleod 1982, 38.

47. T. S. Eliot, 'Tradition and the individual talent', in *Selected Essays* (London, 1932), 13–22.

48. *Poetics* 23, 24; Hor. *Ars Poetica* 136f.; but note Garvie 1994, 10–11.

49. See W. Arend, *Die typischen Scenen bei Homer* (*Problemata* 7, Berlin 1933), with M. Parry's review repr. in 1971, 404–7; Hainsworth 1969, 25–6; bibl. given by E.-R. Schwinge in Latacz 1991, 485.

50. Fenik 1968, 1974; also e.g. Krischer 1971, and Edwards in a series of papers, mostly listed in the bibl. to Edwards 1987. For hospitality-scenes see now S. Reece, *The Stranger's Welcome: Oral Theory and the Aesthetics of the Homeric Hospitality Scene* (Michigan, 1993).

51. J. I. Armstrong, 'The arming motif in the *Iliad*', *AJP* 79 (1958), 337–54; for another aspect see C. Segal, 'Andromache's Anagnorisis', *HSCP* 75 (1971), 33–57.

52. See e.g. J. A. Notopoulos, 'Parataxis in Homer: a new approach to Homeric literary criticism', *TAPA* 80 (1949), 1–23; A. B. Lord, 'Homer as Oral poet', *HSCP* 72 (1967), 1–46 (for his other papers see the bibl. in Lord 1991). A more moderate position is adopted by J. B. Hainsworth, 'The Criticism of an Oral Homer', *JHS* 90 (1970), 90–8 = Wright 1978, 28–40 = Emlyn-Jones et al. 1992, 65–75.

53. Note M. W. M. Pope, 'The Parry-Lord Theory of Homeric Composition', *Acta Classica* 6 (1963), 1–21; A. Hoekstra, *Homeric Modifications of Formulaic Prototypes* (Amsterdam, 1965), ch. 1; D. Young, 'Never blotted a line? Formula and premeditation in Homer and Hesiod', *Arion* 6 (1967), 279–324 = *Essays on Classical Literature selected from Arion*, ed. N. Rudd (Cambridge, 1972), 33–78; W. Whallon, *Formula, Character and Context* (Cambridge, Mass., 1969); A. Parry 1972 = 1989, 301–26; Austin 1975, ch. 1; D. Shive, *Naming Achilles* (New York and Oxford, 1987); N. J. Richardson, 'The individuality of Homer's language', in Bremer et al. 1987, 165–84. See also the discussions cited by A. Parry in M. Parry 1971, xxxiii and xlix n. 3.

54. W. Sale, 'Achilles and Heroic Values', *Arion* 2 (1963), 86–100, J. Russo, 'Homer against his tradition', *Arion* 7 (1968), 275–95 = Latacz 1979, 403–26 (German version), Tsagarakis 1982, esp. 32ff.; cf. Taplin 1992. On technical aspects of the evolution of the formulaic system see J. B. Hainsworth, 'The Homeric Formula and the Problem of its Transmission', *BICS* 9 (1962), 57–68; 'Good and Bad Formulae' in Fenik 1978, 41–50; and esp. the magisterial account in Hainsworth 1993, 1–31; also M. Finkelberg, 'Formulaic and Nonformulaic elements in Homer', *CP* 84 (1989), 179–97. For a different approach, see E. Visser, *Homerische Versificationstechnik* (Frankfurt, 1987); id., 'Formulae or single words? Towards a new theory on Homeric verse-making', *WJA* 14 (1988), 21–37.

55. For Parry's fullest defence of the statement that the meaning of the epithets was unimportant see 1971, 118–72; cf. the briefer account at 304–7. But Parry himself allowed for some cases of deliberate choice or adjustment (1971, 156–61), and the argument is taken further by Hainsworth 1969, 29–30; Macleod 1982, 35–42; Rutherford 1992, 49–57. For Penelope's fat hand see Woodhouse 1930, 20–1, who wails 'Oh Homer! How could you?'; defended by Austin 1975, 73.

56. Griffin 1986, with de Jong 1988; de Jong 1987; Martin 1989; Griffin 1995, 36–45.

57. M. Parry 1971, chh. 13–17 (17 by A. B. Lord), with intro. by A. Parry, xxxiv–xli, xlvii–liii; Lord 1960. See further Finnegan 1977; B. Fenik, *Homer and the Nibelungenlied* (Cambridge Mass., 1986); Hainsworth 1993, 32–53 (valuable essay on 'The *Iliad* as heroic poetry') and for broadening of the comparative picture e.g. Hatto 1980, and other works cited by Hainsworth, loc. cit., and by Taplin 1992, 26 n. 24. A wide-ranging new study in this field is Nagy 1996 (forthcoming from Cambridge).

58. As is over-eagerly attempted by Kirk 1962, 95 ff. Contrast R. Thomas, *Literacy and Orality in Ancient Greece* (Cambridge, 1993), ch. 3.

59. A. B. Lord, 'Homer's Originality: Oral Dictated Texts', *TAPA* 84 (1953), 124–33, and elsewhere; accepted e.g. by Janko 1992, 37–8.

60. A view championed by Bowra 1930, and by Adam Parry (esp. 'Have we Homer's *Iliad?*', *YCS* 20 (1966), 177–216 = A. Parry 1989, 104–40), but one which has had less support in recent years (contrast e.g. Taplin 1992, 8–9, 35–7); see Garvie 1994, 16 n. 51, for a list of those (including myself) who still hold to this theory.

61. B. B. Powell, *Homer and the Origins of the Greek Alphabet* (Cambridge, 1991).

62. Jeffery 1961, 1–42 with addenda on pp. 425–7 in 1990 edn. by Johnston, against the early dating proposed by near-eastern experts such as J. Naveh; Burkert 1992, 25–33. See also A. Heubeck, *Schrift* (Arch. Homerica 10, Göttingen, 1979); Thomas (see n. 58 above).

63. Cost: *IG* i³ 476, 289f.; cf. Jeffery 1961, 56–7; Jensen 1980, 94 ff. Burkert (see last n.) supports leather.

64. On Homeridai, Pind. *Nem.* 2. 1–5 and scholia; Pl. *Ion* 530d, *Rep.* 10. 599e; see further Allen 1924, 42–50; W. Burkert, 'Die Leistung eines Kreophylos: Kreophyleer, Homeriden und die archaische Heraklesepik', *MH* 29 (1972), 74–85; D. Fehling, 'Zwei Lehrstücke über Pseudo-Nachrichten (Homeriden, Lelantischer Krieg)', *RhM* 122 (1979), 193–210 (total scepticism).

65. *WD* 650–9; M. L. West, *Hesiod, Theogony* (Oxford, 1966), 40–8, with criticisms by G. P. Edwards, *The Language of Hesiod* (Oxford, 1971), 199–206; Janko 1982, 94–8.

66. M. L. West, 'Greek Poetry 2000–700 B.C.', *CQ* 23 (1973), 179–92, at 191–2; G. P. Edwards (see last n.), ch. 8; Rutherford on xix. 111, 203. More generally on Hesiod in comparison with Homer see H. T. Wade-Gery, 'Hesiod', *Essays on Greek History* (Oxford, 1959), ch. 1; Murray 1980 (revised 1993), chh. 3–4; P. Millett, 'Hesiod and his world', *PCPS* n.s. 30 (1984), 84–115.

67. These are in the OCT Homer, vol. 5; also in the recent editions of epic fragments by Bernabé (Leipzig, 1988) and Davies (Göttingen, 1988). For discussion see A. Severyns, *Recherches sur la Chrestomathie de Proclos* (Paris, 1938–63); G. L. Huxley, *Greek Epic Poetry from Eumelos to Panyassis* (London, 1969); Griffin 1977; M. Davies, *The Epic Cycle* (Bristol, 1987).

68. Callim. *epigr.* 28 Pfeiffer, Hor. *Ars* 132, 136; Pfeiffer 1968, 227–30.

69. On the hymn to Demeter, N. J. Richardson, *The Homeric Hymn to Demeter* (Oxford, 1974), and H. Foley (ed.), *The Homeric Hymn to Demeter* (Princeton, 1994); on the hymns generally, Janko 1982 (very technical), Thalmann 1984, J. S. Clay, *The Politics of Olympus: Form and Meaning in the Major Homeric Hymns* (Princeton, 1989), and R. Parker, 'The Hymn to Demeter and the Homeric Hymns', *G&R* 38 (1991), 1–17.

70. See J. A. Davison, 'Quotations and allusions in early Greek literature', *Eranos* 53 (1955), 125–40 = Davison, *From Archilochus to Pindar* (London, 1968), 70–85, a classic statement of this argument. The same question arises with the well-known inscription from Pithecusae, describing the artefact it adorns as 'Nestor's cup' (R. Meiggs–D. Lewis, *A Selection of Greek Historical Inscriptions* (Oxford, 1969, rev. 1988), no. 1; P. A. Hansen, *Carmina Epigraphica Graeca* i (Berlin 1983), 454): is the cup a stock item in the epic tradition, or does this indicate knowledge of *Iliad* 11. 632–7?

71. Alcman *PMG* 77 and 80; Alcaeus F 44 Lobel-Page; Stesich. *SLG* esp. S11, revised in M. Davies, *Poetarum melicorum graecorum fragmenta* i (Oxford, 1991), cf. D. L. Page, 'Stesichorus, *Geryoneis*', *JHS* 93 (1973), 138–54. On the dating of Stesichorus, M. L. West, 'Stesichorus', *CQ* 21 (1971), 302–14; D. A. Campbell, *Greek Lyric* iii (Loeb edn., Harvard 1991), 2–4; see further Burkert 1987.

72. K. F. Johansen, *The Iliad in Early Greek Art* (Copenhagen, 1967); O. Touchefeu-Meynier, *Thèmes odysséens dans l'art antique* (Paris, 1968); R. Kannicht, 'Poetry and Art: Homer and the Monuments Afresh', *ClAntiq* 1 (1982), 70–86; F. Brommer, *Odysseus: die Taten und Leiden des Helden in antiker Kunst und Literatur* (Darmstadt, 1983); C. Brillante, 'Episodi iliadici nell'arte figurata', *RhM* 126 (1983), 97–125; T. H. Carpenter, *Art and Myth in Ancient Greece* (London, 1991). For the *Odyssey* see also D. Buitron et al., *The Odyssey and Ancient Art: an epic in word and image* (Edith C. Blum Art Inst., Annandale-on-Hudson, N.Y., 1992); compare also D. Buitron-Oliver and B. Cohen, 'Between Skylla and Penelope; female characters of the *Odyssey* in archaic and classical Greek art', in Cohen

1995, 29–58 (with 60 illustrations in the following pages). Authoritative essays are now provided for individual characters in the *Lexicon Iconographicum Mythologiae Classicae* (Zurich-Munich 1981–).

73. For example, the long-standing debate over the presence of hoplite-tactics in the *Iliad*, on which see recently H. van Wees, 'Kings in combat: battles and heroes in the *Iliad*', *CQ* 38 (1992), 1–24 (pro) and Janko on 13. 126–35 (con). See generally G. S. Kirk, 'Objective dating criteria in Homer', *MH* 17 (1960), 189–205 = Kirk 1964, 174–90.

74. 9. 404–5, with C. Morgan, *Athletes and Oracles: The Transformation of Olympia and Delphi in the Eighth Century B.C.* (Cambridge, 1990), 106 ff. The arguments of W. Burkert, 'Das hunderttorige Theben und die Datierung der Ilias', *WS* n.s. 10 (1976), 5–21, that the *Iliad* must postdate 715 or even belong in the seventh century, based on the reference to Egyptian Thebes in the same speech, are rejected by Janko 1992, 14 n. 20, and by Graham in Cohen 1995, 5.

75. Janko 1982, 195–6, 200, 228–32 puts it at the early extreme, but allows some margin for error. A provocative paper by M. L. West in *Mus. Helv.* 52 (1995) questions the validity of chronology based on statistics, and offers new arguments for dating the *Iliad* in the mid-600s.

76. Burkert 1987 puts it rather later, in the last quarter of the sixth century.

77. Pl. *Hipparchus* 228b, Isoc. *Paneg.* 159, Lycurgus 1. 102, Cic. *de or.* 3. 137; Janko 1992, 29 ff.; R. Merkelbach, 'Die Pisistratische Redaktion der homerischen Gedichte', *RhM* 95 (1952), 23–47 = *Untersuchungen zur Odyssee* (2nd edn. Munich, 1969), 239–62; J. A. Davison, 'Peisistratos and Homer', *TAPA* 86 (1955), 1–21; D. M. Lewis, *CAH* iv², 292. For a different approach see G. Nagy, 'An evolutionary model for the making of Homeric poetry: comparative perspectives', in *The Ages of Homer* (see n. 4 above), 163–79; he sees the story of the Pisistratean recension as in effect a myth describing a gradual process by which the text became fixed.

78. Jensen 1980, esp. ch. 7.

79. Hes. fr. 357 M-W seems to anticipate the image, but applying it to the bard; ctr. Pind. *Nem.* 2.2. See H. Patzer, 'Rhapsodos', *Hermes* 80 (1952), 314–24; R. Sealey, 'From Phemius to Ion', *REG* 70 (1957), 17–46; Herington 1985, 167–76; Burkert 1987.

80. For the emergence of interpretation of Homer by non-poets see the Derveni papyrus (*ZPE* 47, 1982, at end); Ar. *Banqueters* fr. 233 K-A; Prt. 80A29, 30; Plut. *Alcib.* 7.1. See Richardson 1975.

81. See esp. Hainsworth's 1993 commentary; earlier bibl. on his p. 155, esp. F. Klingner, 'Über die Dolonie', *Hermes* 75 (1940), 337–68 = *Studien zur griechischen und römischen Literatur* (Zürich, 1964), 7–39, W. Danek, *Studien zur Dolonie* (*WS* Beiheft 12, Vienna 1988).

82. Other cases are for the most part much shorter. In antiquity there were controversies about so-called Athenian interpolations (Arist. *Rhet.* 1375b30, Dieuchidas 485F6 = D. L. 1. 57; cf. Allen 1924, 241 ff.), but the Athenians make so small a showing in the *Iliad* that it is hard to suppose that much was added. Suspect passages on this score include 1. 265, 2. 553–5, xi. 631. On manuscript evidence for interpolation see G. M. Bolling, *The External Evidence for Interpolation in Homer* (Oxford, 1925) and M. J. Apthorp, *The Manuscript Evidence for Interpolation in Homer* (Heidelberg, 1980): the problems are too complex to discuss here.

83. The expression derives from a famous line in Horace's *Ars Poetica*, in which the Roman poet admits that literary perfection, however desirable, is not always attainable: 'et idem/ indignor quandoque bonus dormitat Homerus,/ verum operi longo fas est obrepere somnum' (*Ars* 358–60: 'I even feel aggrieved, when good Homer nods; but when a work is long, a drowsy mood is understandable'). Pope's riposte to this tag should be taken seriously by critics: 'Those oft are stratagems which error seem,/ nor is it Homer nods, but we that dream' (*An Essay on Criticism*, 179 f.).

84. Page 1959, 305.

85. On textual criticism in general see M. L. West, *Textual Criticism and Editorial Technique* (Stuttgart, 1973); L. D. Reynolds and N. G. Wilson, *Scribes and Scholars* (1968; 3rd edn., Oxford, 1991), ch. 6; for more detail on the Homeric tradition see J. A. Davison in Wace-Stubbings 1962, 215–33; S. West 1988, 33–48. The 'wild papyri' are edited by S. West, *The Ptolemaic papyri of Homer* (Cologne, 1967); for a brief account see E. G. Turner, *Greek papyri* (1968, 2nd edn. Oxford, 1980), 106–112. Besides the variations in manuscript evidence, there is the supplementary testimony of ancient quotations: for a conspicuous case of a passage preserved only in one source, not represented in mss. or papyri, see 9. 458–61, quoted by Plutarch as excised by Aristarchus; these lines may well be authentic (cf. S. West, 'Crime prevention and ancient editors (*Il.* 9. 458–61)', *LCM* 7 (1982), 84–6, Janko 1992, 27–8; Hainsworth 1993, ad loc.). On the Alexandrian scholars see P. M. Fraser, *Ptolemaic Alexandria* (Oxford, 1972), 447–79; Davison in Wace-Stubbings 1962, 222–6; Pfeiffer 1968, part 2, esp. chh. 2 and 6; Janko 1992, 22–9 (with invaluable bibl. and lists of examples of their judgements).

86. Nagy 1992, esp. 30–1; Seaford 1994, 144–54, part of a complex argument many stages of which I cannot accept. Griffin 1995, 8 [marred by an unfortunate large-scale misprint] attempts a brief response to Seaford. See also Sourvinou-Inwood 1995, 94–103.

87. W. Burkert, *Greek Religion* (Oxford, 1985), 119–25; J. Gould in Hornblower (see n. 13 above), 91–106.

88. See Hornblower (see last n.) 6 ff. for historiography; L. Radermacher, *Artium Scriptores. Reste der voraristotelischen Rhetorik* (Vienna, 1951), 1–10 for rhetoric. Satyrus, *Life of Euripides* fr. 39, col. vii, 23 ff. Arrighetti, comments on the line of descent from Homer to New Comedy. Homer as Ocean: Quintil. 10.1.46; F. Williams's commentary on Callimachus, *Hymn to Apollo*, pp. 98–9.

89. Solon F 29 West, Hes. *Theog.* 27–8; Thalmann 1984, 147–9; L. H. Pratt, *Lying and Poetry from Homer to Pindar* (Ann Arbor, Michigan, 1993).

90. Cf. E. R. Curtius, *European Literature and the Latin Middle Ages* (Eng. tr.; London 1953), ch. 11.

91. A. S. Pease on Cic. *On the Nature of the Gods* 1. 42.

92. Cf. P. E. Easterling, 'The Tragic Homer', *BICS* 31 (1984), 1–8; S. Goldhill, *Reading Greek Tragedy* (Cambridge, 1986), esp. ch. 6.

93. For mutual rivalry and criticism among poets see e.g. Simonides on Pittacus, *PMG* 542, and on Cleobulus, ibid. 581; also the stories of a contest between Homer and Hesiod. See further M. Griffith, 'Contest and contradiction in early Greek Poetry', in M. Griffith and D. Mastronarde (ed.), *Cabinet of the Muses* (New York, 1990), 185–207; R. G. A. Buxton, *Imaginary Greece* (Cambridge, 1994), 31.

94. Pfeiffer 1968 is the fundamental reference-work, supplemented by Richardson 1975, and esp. 1993, 25–49. See also Lamberton-Keaney 1992.

95. *Hom. Probl.*: frr. 142–79 Rose. *Poetics* 25, with commentaries; M. Carroll, *Aristotle's Poetics Ch. XXV in the light of the Homeric Scholia* (Baltimore, 1885).

96. *Poetics* 25. 1460b13–21, tr. M. Hubbard (slightly modified). See further S. Halliwell, *Aristotle's Poetics* (London, 1986), 10–17 and ch. 7.

97. For the Hellenistic critics whose views are quoted by the scholia see the works cited in n. 85 above; also Kirk 1985, 38–43; R. Meijering, *Literary and Rhetorical Theories in Greek Scholia* (Groningen, 1987).

98. The monumental edition of most of the scholia to the *Iliad* is by H. Erbse (Berlin and N.Y., 1969–88), though for the mythological commentaries, and for the *Odyssey*, one must still go back to Dindorf's edition. For guidance on their critical criteria and preoccupations Richardson 1980 is invaluable. Cf. Richardson 1993, 35 ff.; see also M. Heath, *Unity in Greek Poetics* (Oxford, 1989), ch. 8. Griffin 1980 also makes use of the scholia, but tends to praise or damn them according to the extent that they confirm his views.

99. Richardson 1980, 283–7; Edwards 1987, ch. 15.

100. Finley 1954 (rev. 1978) and Redfield 1975 are particularly important works in this area; more recently, van Wees 1992; see also two long and fully-documented essays by Raaflaub, in Latacz 1991 and Hansen 1993.

101. W. Burkert, *Greek Religion* (Eng. tr. Oxford, 1985) is a rich store of insights (cf. E. Kearns' review, *JHS* 107, 1987, 215–18). See also R. Parker, *Miasma: Pollution and Purification in Early Greek Religion* (Oxford, 1983), 66 ff., 130 ff. etc.; Griffin 1980, chh. 5–6; new ch. in Redfield 1975 (revised edn.). See further pp. 44 ff. below. For a more general study of the problems of interpreting Greek religion from the outside, see E. Kearns, 'Order, interaction, authority ...', in *The Greek World*, ed. A. Powell (London, 1995), 511–29.

102. Edwards 1987, chh. 11–14; Griffin 1980, ch. 1. Rather differently Lynn-George 1988, e.g. 252–72 on grave-mounds and monuments. On metaphor see M. Parry 1971, 365–75, 414–18; C. Moulton, 'Homeric metaphor', *CPh* 74 (1979), 279–93; Edwards 1991, 48–53. For a bold new approach see D. Lateiner, *Sardonic Smile: Nonverbal behavior in Homeric Epic* (Ann Arbor, Michigan, 1995).

103. G. Genette, *Narrative Discourse* (Eng. tr. London, 1980), M. Bal, *Narratology* (Toronto, 1985).

104. Pragmatic treatment in Griffin 1986; more theoretically grounded, de Jong 1987, 1991, and other papers; S. Richardson, *The Homeric Narrator* (Nashville, 1990). See also Edwards 1991, intr. 1–10; V. di Benedetto, *Nel laboratorio di Omero* (Turin, 1994) part 1.

II. THE *ILIAD*[1]

Structure, Characterization, Themes

The *Iliad* is not an *Achilleid*, although Achilles is the most important character in the epic. One of the most striking features of the poem is the way in which it embraces the action of the whole Trojan war by retrospective and prospective references, rather than by narrating the events in full. In this, as is evident from ancient testimony, the *Iliad* was markedly different from the 'cyclic' epics (see esp. Hor. *Ars* 136f.). The human characters refer to the abduction of Helen, the initial embassy to the Trojans, the mustering at Aulis, the earlier campaigns and clashes; the prophecies and comments of the gods, particularly Zeus and Thetis, anticipate the doom of Achilles and the ultimate fall of Troy, also grimly foreshadowed in other ways.[2] In an important passage which seems to be deliberately reserved for a late stage in the poem, Homer himself looks back to the origin of the whole conflict, the judgement of Paris which aroused the implacable anger of Athena and Hera against Troy.[3] Another remarkable feature is the intensity of the action of the poem. In terms of time, the whole poem occupies some 40 days, of which only 14 include narrated events, and three in particular are the subject of fourteen books.[4] As for place, the human action is virtually confined to three areas: the camp of the Greeks, the city of Troy, and the plain of battle which lies between. The scenes involving the Olympians are more various and provide a broader perspective, but their attention too is generally focussed on the human suffering on the battlefield. Consequently the *Iliad* gains in emotional power what it lacks in diversity of scene and situation. A third feature, already implied, is the prominence of the Trojans in the poem. The very title *Iliad*, though probably not original, reminds us that this is no jingoistic or 'pan-Hellenic' epic; despite the claims of some ancient commentators, the Trojans are treated by Homer with great sympathy and generosity.[5] That is not to deny the fundamental guilt of Paris or to assert that the Achaean victory is undeserved.

The main subject of the poem is proclaimed as the wrath of Achilles. Much remains undisclosed by the opening lines in which the poet states his theme. In particular, we are given no hint that the anger of the hero will change direction: having first been directed against Agamemnon and his fellow-Greeks, it will be turned after Patroclus' death far more savagely against the Trojans and above all against Hector. Moreover, the way in which the hero's wrath ends proves to be as important as the punishment of his enemies. Rather than making Achilles relent as a result of compensation or apology, Homer allows violent revenge to give way to pity and magnanimity. Heroic wrath itself is clearly a traditional theme,[6] and on the evidence of the formulaic system it is likely that Achilles and Hector had both figured in epic for a long period before the *Iliad*,[7] but it is not so clear whether the tale of Achilles' anger had been narrated before Homer. At any rate, the conception of Achilles as a proud, intransigent yet ultimately noble figure is central to the plot of the *Iliad*, and it is surely the *Iliad* which made Achilles no mere rebellious chief but a tragic figure, remote from his fellow-heroes and mysterious to them, caught half-way between divinity and humanity, doomed to an early end, hungry for glory yet seeing at times its elusiveness and even its futility.

The main plot-line of the *Iliad*, then, is inevitably the sequence involving Achilles' withdrawal from the war and his reactions to the Greeks' overtures and subsequent events. At least the first half of the poem is dominated by his absence; in book 9 the Greeks unsuccessfully beg him to return; in book 11 a long and intricate process begins which culminates in Patroclus' more successful appeal in book 16, an appeal which leads to the latter's death. Thereafter Achilles' return to battle is inevitable, but characteristically delayed (the well-known Homeric fondness for 'retardation') – first by the time-lapse until he receives the news, then by the need for fresh armour, then by the formal reconciliation with Agamemnon. Thereafter the spotlight is on Achilles, who on re-entering the battle carries all before him, and who dominates the last six books of the poem. Heroic revenge is achieved in book 22, with the slaying of Hector. It has often been maintained that the poem could have ended at this point, with the hero triumphant and the Greeks certain of their future victory. Whatever the truth about earlier versions of the tale, it is difficult to believe that the poet who has throughout shown Hector and his fellow-Trojans in such an attractive light would have abandoned the Trojan hero to the atrocities of Achilles and denied him burial. A further argument comes from the character of Achilles himself. The friend of Patroclus, the man who showed respect for the father of Andromache, the sparer of suppliants in earlier times, the most emotional and articulate, yet most impulsive speaker in the poem, is no killing-machine. The final scenes of the poem including the hero, those between Achilles and Priam, allow gentler feelings to surface and provide a foil to the savagery which has gone before. Verbal and thematic echoes seem to confirm that the 24th book is a carefully integrated conclusion to the *Iliad*.[8]

Much that is contained in the *Iliad* is only tangentially connected with the main story-line. Hence the analysts sought to identify an 'original' wrath-poem, usually regarding certain books as essential to this narrative (esp. 1, 16 and 22),[9] while rejecting others as later additions. The alternative model, now more fashionable, regards the *Iliad* as a creative synthesis, drawing on material which had been previously separate but combining episodes and sequences of events into a greater whole. On this assumption, we may accept that some planks in the structure were originally independent, but we may still see the new combination as harmonious and effective. The adaptation is not always perfect: it is fairly clear that the Catalogue of Achaean forces in book 2 has been adapted from a poem in which it featured at the beginning of the expedition: in particular, whereas a catalogue of ships makes sense at that earlier point, when the fleet assembled at Aulis, there is little point in listing the number of ships so late in the war, without considering the number of men who survive. The editorial hand is particularly clear in the short passages which adapt the catalogue to changed circumstances, explaining the death of Protesilaus and the absence of Philoctetes.[10]

This approach seems preferable in considering, for example, the early books in which the Greeks try to maintain their superiority without Achilles. In the hero's absence, other characters (Menelaus, Nestor, Odysseus) take the limelight: in particular, Homer gives special prominence to Diomedes, a hero of great courage and energy, but one who lacks the hot temper and self-destructive tendencies of Achilles, and who functions as a foil to the greater hero. Diomedes enjoys an *aristeia* in books 5 and 6: that is, a period in battle in which he shows himself to be 'best' (*aristos*) and fights with exceptional success. Much that he says and does there, interesting and exciting in itself, stands in contrast with Achilles' behaviour in his later and more extraordinary *aristeia*, in books 20 to 22.[11] This is characteristic of Homer's technique: the heroes do not exist in isolation, but are regularly compared or contrasted with one another. Achilles and Patroclus (book 16), Hector and Paris (books 3 and 6), Hector and Polydamas (18. 249–314), Odysseus and Menelaus (3. 205–24), Odysseus and Achilles (19. 145–237), are a few examples.

Because his poem is an *Iliad* and not an *Achilleid*, Homer includes many other heroes and gives them their share of glory. Diomedes has already been mentioned; the Cretan heroes Idomeneus and Meriones are prominent in book 13, Patroclus has his brief hour of glory in book 16, and the greater Ajax, typically excelling in defence, plays a key part in blocking the Trojan onslaught on the ships (books 15 and 16). Even Agamemnon, though shown in no very favourable light by Homer, has a somewhat abbreviated *aristeia* in book 11 until he is wounded. Defenders of book 10 might wish to see it as an atypical *aristeia* (at night, and involving spying and trickery) suitable for the crafty Odysseus. After the fighting of the *Iliad* has come to an end, the funeral games held by Achilles for Patroclus are used by the poet to show the various heroes in action once more, but in lighter vein: Taplin has described the episode as a 'curtain-call'. The contests of the games show the Greeks contending with each other, in pursuit of honour and prizes as on the battlefield, but with less deadly consequences.[12] All of this implies an audience familiar with these characters and eager to see them play their part in an unusually ambitious epic.

Not much has been said so far about the Trojans and the scenes within the city (esp. books 3, 6, 22, 24); yet these are among the most memorable aspects of the poem.[13] While it was natural that in a poem of this scale much should be seen of the warriors on both sides, it was not inevitable that the Trojans, particularly Hector, should be portrayed with such sympathy. In book 24 Helen stresses Hector's gentleness, and that of his father Priam: it is obvious that these qualities, illustrated in books 3 and 6, were important to the poet's conception of these major characters.[14] The household of Hector, with loving wife and infant son for whom his father hopes for so much in vain, epitomizes the civilized life of the city which the Greeks will destroy; moreover, the family life of Hector stands in contrast with the isolated individualism of Achilles, whose son Neoptolemus is mentioned only once, as the son of a war-bride being brought up far away, and whose feelings for Briseis, the cause of the quarrel, veer from possessiveness to exaggerated affection and later to animosity. If Achilles shows us what a supreme hero, son of a goddess, is like, Hector embodies a more human ideal: a warrior who fights not just for glory but to protect his family and his fellow-citizens.[15] The vain and frivolous Paris, an archer and generally an unheroic figure, is perfectly contrasted with the more sombre and serious Hector; the adverse judgement and taunting comments of Helen reveal the disharmony that reigns in their household, where there is no child and no true marriage. Yet Paris can rally and behave well when rebuked by his brother, and is later prominent in battle: though he may be 'the archetypal Trojan', he is not contemptible.[16] Finally, Priam, who is too old to fight and in some episodes cuts a curiously ineffective figure, rises to a genuinely heroic level of determination and courage when he journeys by night, at the risk of his life, to beg Achilles for Hector's corpse. The wonder and compassion which Achilles feels, and the way in which the two men sit gazing in admiration at one another, guide the audience's response (24.

483, 516, 628–34). Suffering and endurance of loss are part of the heroic life as well as victory and slaughter.[17]

Returning to principles of structure, some generalizations may be offered, most of which will recur at a later stage. We have seen that Homeric poetry is characterized by repetition on both a verbal and a thematic level; situations recur, on a large and on a small scale, and are described in the same or comparable ways. If variations are introduced, these are often important. One striking case of a small-scale episode which provides a parallel to the main plot of the poem concerns a minor character, Euchenor, the son of a prophet. He was warned by his father that he had a choice of lives: either he could die of a slow and cruel disease at home, or else in battle at Troy. He chose the latter, and is slain by Paris in book 13 (660–72). The motif of the choice of lives is used on a grander scale with Achilles, especially in book 9: since the choice of a long illness is an easier one to reject, the poet makes the alternative more tempting: a long life of prosperity and comfort in his native land – but without glory (9. 410–16).

Another case concerns the origins of the quarrel and of the war itself. The Greeks have come to Troy because of the abduction of a woman, Helen, after peaceful efforts have failed to recover her; the priest Chryses calls down Apollo's retribution on the Greeks because Agamemnon has seized his daughter Chryseis, after his own efforts to reclaim her have failed; and Achilles denounces Agamemnon and withdraws from the war because the king has deprived him of his prize, Briseis. The analogy between the two slave-girls is particularly clear from the parallelism of name. The poet composed naturally in such patterns.[18]

The *Iliad* achieves its vast length partly by elaboration of episodes, partly by retardation. On the whole, the more important an episode, the more fully it is narrated, usually with the addition of speeches and similes. Thus the advance of the Achaean forces in book 2 is adorned with no fewer than four similes. When an important warrior is about to embark on an *aristeia*, he is often given an arming-scene; the most extensive such scene is that of Achilles, for whom new armour is actually manufactured by the gods. When a major duel is to be fought, the gods observe and comment; their attention enhances the significance of an event. Often a less significant or less emotional incident will precede and prepare for a greater: thus the attack by Diomedes on Aphrodite can be seen as a more humorous, less formidable anticipation of the attack on Ares.[19] On a larger scale the whole episode of Diomedes' attack on the gods, which has no tragic consequences, is a prefiguration of the more momentous battle between Achilles and the River-god. From one point of view these sequences show the poet manipulating formulaic or traditional material, but he is in control of his techniques and resources, not deploying them at random.

As for retardation, this is conspicuous in both epics on both a large and a small scale. The promise of Zeus to Thetis in book 1 is not even referred to again for several books, and he only begins to go to work in book 8; the return of Achilles to the field is anticipated as early as book 9, becomes imminent in book 16, but does not actually take place until book 20. The urgent message of Nestor to Achilles is delayed while Patroclus pauses to tend Eurypylus (11. 809–48, taken up at 15. 390–404). Similarly in specific episodes: in book 16 the narrator has made it clear that Patroclus is doomed, and we are shown Zeus looking down on the combat, pondering over the hero's fate: will he strike him down now, or allow him a little longer, a few more moments of deluded triumph? The god, here a mirror-image of the poet, chooses the latter (644–55). As in Attic tragedy, the audience relishes the suspense while aware of the inevitable outcome; what is in doubt is not so much what will happen, but when it will happen.[20]

As the last example suggests, Homer makes extensive use of foreshadowing, whether explicit (as in the prophecy of a god or a comment by the omniscient narrator) or implicit (as in the symbolic moment where Patroclus must leave behind Achilles' spear, which he cannot lift: like other details in that scene, this suggests that he is no adequate substitute for Achilles).[21] Major prophecies by Zeus foretell subsequent events and map out the course of the poem (8. 470–7, 15. 49–77); narrative commentary on misguided hopes or unfulfilled prayers provide irony and poignancy (e.g. 16. 249–52). Other forms of intervention by the narrator include invocations (usually at powerful moments) and résumés; also noteworthy are the frequent occasions where we are told that an event *nearly* happened, but (e.g.) a quick intervention by a god averted this outcome.[22] But at this point study of narrative technique merges into more detailed analysis of style, which cannot be attempted here.

Major episodes in the Homeric poems are frequently linked in some way other than by explicit cross-reference. Important parallels connect the parting of Hector and Andromache, and other moments in book 6, with the passage in book 22 in which Andromache learns of her husband's death. Similarly Thetis' appearance in book 18 in response to her son's grief is a mirror-scene, a repetition of the moment in which she came to comfort him for a far less important loss in book 1; verbal parallels reinforce the connection. The analogies between the death-scenes of Patroclus and Hector are well-known: the parallels are too prominent, the occasions too important, for these to be coincidental.[23] The sequence of scenes involving exchanges between Hector and Polydamas lead up to the climactic moment of wise advice ignored in book 18.[24] Above all, the scene in book 24 in which Priam successfully appeals to Achilles seems to cap and surpass the embassy-scene in book 9. In both, Achilles receives an unexpected visit by night; in both, he is offered rich compensation; in both, food and drink are consumed (though in book 24 only after the appeal has succeeded); and in both, Achilles gives a passionate statement of his disillusionment. The differences are of course equally significant: Priam, a king, has come face to face with Achilles as Agamemnon did not (cf. esp. 9. 372–3, 387, with 24. 519–21); he has brought the treasure with him, rather than merely sending a catalogue; he humbles himself far more than the Greek ambassadors, and approaches Achilles at far greater risk.[25] As for Achilles, his self-centred eloquence in book 9 has given way to a more sombre and compassionate mood in 24, and although still bitter and quick to anger, he is able to see the parallels between his own and Priam's situations.[26]

Something has been said about structure and characterization. A more nebulous concept is that of the poem's 'theme' or themes, as distinct from the plot. The term is sometimes used for the recurring motifs or typical episodes in Homeric epic (thus an arming-scene might be an instance of a theme),[27] but here I use it in a different sense, found in analysis of literary as well as oral texts. In this context, the term refers to the larger abstract, moral or metaphysical issues which seem to be implied or to arise out of the text. With a work as long and complex as the *Iliad*, this raises problems: must we insist on specifying a single theme for the whole, and if not, how many themes are to be allowed? Kirk is hostile towards 'single-minded interpretations in terms of tragic essence or human predicament',[28] and there is some risk of losing contact with the particularities of the poem. Nevertheless, it is natural to want to go beyond mere re-telling of the story, and we are on relatively safe ground in considering the issues which seem to matter most to, and to be most extensively debated by, the characters themselves. Conduct in war, the winning of honour, the rights and wrongs of the quarrel and of the war itself, the justice of the gods, and the morality of victory, matter greatly to Homer's heroes and presumably to the poet and his society. The privileged access which the audience is allowed to the counsels of the gods also helps us to assess the overall import of the story, though the divine perspective raises questions as well as answering them. In the sections which follow I shall discuss three major topics: warfare, men's relation to the gods, and human error or folly. I shall try to describe the way in which the poet presents these themes and to draw out some of the possible implications for an Iliadic view of the world.[29]

War and the hero

Already in the proem we are told that we must expect violent death in battle; the Achaean and Trojan hosts are marshalled for combat in book 2; wholehearted conflict begins at the close of book 4, and warfare dominates most of the poem up to the climax of Hector's death in book 22. Even the most memorable scenes off the battlefield – the meeting of Hector and Andromache, the embassy, the Olympian episodes, Nestor's lecture to Patroclus – are overshadowed by the war, and their outcome often influences its progress. The fighting of the *Iliad* has been much studied: some of this work has concentrated on the formulaic and thematic construction of the battle-scenes, while other scholars have discussed the relation of this poetic fighting to real-life tactics and warfare of the Dark Age. Finally, there has been intense discussion of the ideology of the war in the *Iliad*, and of the attitudes of the poet and his characters to the slaughter which the poem relentlessly narrates.

The fighting in the *Iliad* involves large forces on both sides, but the focus is constantly narrowing to describe the exploits of individuals, usually in one-to-one combat. The leaders organize formal duels in books 3 and 7 (Menelaus vs. Paris, Ajax vs. Hector), and in book 22 Achilles will permit no-one else to share his revenge upon Hector; but even in books which represent a general battle-scene the poet normally prefers to follow the progress of particular heroes, whether major figures of the poem or lesser characters temporarily given the limelight. True, there are passages which take a broader view, and similes sometimes describe the clash of opposing armies, but the main narrative focusses on individuals. Moreover, this is aristocratic combat: the common man is almost invisible.[30] In book 2 Odysseus rebukes any noisy slacker of the lower ranks: 'you are of no account in war or in counsel' (202). Thersites, their clownish spokesman, gets a beating for daring to question his betters.[31] Although numerous characters are introduced, and no doubt often invented, to die in battle, the poet in his introductions usually makes them of at least respectable birth. In a bizarre passage, Thoas even recommends that the Achaeans send the common troops back to the ships, 'and let us, who can claim to be the best men among the host, stand firm' (15. 294–9). His advice is followed: in a crisis, it seems, one is actually better off without the lower ranks.

There are many other respects in which the warfare of the *Iliad* is highly unrealistic, even if we set aside the numerous interventions by the gods for later discussion. The army of the Achaeans has been at Troy for nine years, yet only after a setback in book 7 of the poem is a defensive wall constructed around the camp (this aspect also perplexed Thucydides, who gave a different account of events on *a priori* grounds, 1. 11).[32] The sources of supplies for so vast an army are never fully clarified: the most explicit hint is the arrival late in book 7 of a fleet of ships from Lemnos bringing fresh wine.[33] There seems to be no concept of a supporting staff of carpenters, smiths, oarsmen or other camp-followers to handle practical matters: the heroes themselves perform all such tasks, and the army apparently contains no non-combatants. The physician Machaon is wounded in 11. 504–15, and in the absence of his fellow-doctor Podalirius he has to be treated by amateurs (11. 618ff.; cf. Eurypylus, 11. 828–36). Even the aged Nestor is still active at least in advising the charioteers on tactics, and sometimes seems even to be participating in the fighting (4. 322–3, cf. 8. 80ff., 11. 500–1); still more surprising is the appearance of old Phoenix as commander of one of the columns of the Myrmidons (16. 196).[34] There are no slaves except for those (mostly female) taken in war. Little is said about the discomfort of life in camp (though Odysseus allows that separation from their families for so long is indeed hard to bear, 2. 289–97). The weather never varies, and the heroes suffer neither privation nor natural diseases – the exception is of course the plague imposed on them as divine punishment in book 1. The heroes have horses and chariots, which could hardly have been brought *en masse* from mainland Greece by sea; perhaps they are thought to be part of the loot from raids in the Troad mentioned by Achilles and others, for Diomedes captures Aeneas' horses within the poem itself. But the chariots themselves are mysterious vehicles: the poet seems not entirely to grasp their possible function in war, and the heroes use them merely to ride to the battlefield, whereupon they dismount and fight on their feet. Sometimes the concepts of chariot transport and horse-riding are confused: in one notorious passage the Trojan forces try to leap across the Achaean trench, horses, chariots and all! (16. 364ff., cf. 380)[35]

More striking still are the actual clashes between warriors.[36] These follow regular patterns: a common sequence is for a hero to cast a spear, which misses his opponent, and for the opponent to respond with fatal effect. Alternatively, the first shot may miss its intended target but kill another hero close at hand. A chain of killings regularly develops, with a friend of the slain man rallying to avenge his comrade by attacking the slayer. The weapons used are the throwing-spear, the thrusting spear, and the sword; archery, though practised by certain individuals such as Paris and Teucer, is as far as possible marginalized, and the term 'archer' can even be used as an insult (11. 385). Apart from the *Doloneia*, the poem excludes almost entirely any kind of fighting that would involve deception or devices other than hand-to-hand combat.[37] This partly explains the curious way in which the 'disguise' of Patroclus in Achilles' armour is handled: Patroclus is quite clear that the object is 'to make them think I am you' (16. 41), but although this is indeed the initial effect, it is not long before Sarpedon suspects an impostor, and thereafter the idea is dropped: by line 543 Glaucus is in no doubt that the new arrival is Patroclus.[38]

There is a recognized hierarchy of heroes on both sides, though a particular hero's status may be questioned or mockingly challenged in moments of anger. Major heroes slay more people than minor figures; moreover, it is virtually impossible for a minor hero to kill a major figure, and this can only be achieved with the aid of a god (as Apollo will aid Paris in slaying Achilles, 22. 359–60). Success is swift once a hero actually confronts his foe: duels are rarely prolonged beyond a single exchange of shots. If a man is wounded, he either dies at once or is rescued by his allies and recovers. Pain is real but short-lived: the hero may groan deeply, but he does not give way to the agony. Homer does not show his characters delirious or raving in pain (contrast Sophocles, *Philoctetes*, 730–806). If the wound is not severe, careful medical treatment (occasionally with divine intervention) restores him to unblemished health. Only in exceptional cases – Sarpedon, Patroclus, and Hector – can the dying man even speak a few words before the end. Perhaps most strikingly of all, there are no walking wounded: on neither side do we see cripples or other permanently maimed warriors. After battle has ended, the bodies must be recovered and burned with honours: this procedure is carried out with dignity and without gruesome descriptions of the condition of the dead.

All of these conventions serve to create a highly artificial yet curiously convincing world, in which warfare is straightforward and noble.[39] Naturally victory in the war remains the ultimate goal, but in the day-to-day action of the battlefield the most important challenge for each warrior is to face the foe courageously, and if necessary to meet a heroic death. Individual achievement is of greater moment than overall strategy or united planning. Despite the occasional wise pronouncement by Nestor, there is little in the way of tactical discussion before the battle, and next to none when actually on the field. Obligations and duties are conceived on a personal level: naturally one rallies to the aid of a friend or a brother in danger. But the immediate aim is simple: to kill one's opponents until the enemy are put to flight. Beyond that, the Achaeans are fighting for glory and booty, as well as to win back Helen and avenge the insult to Menelaus' honour. The Trojans, whom many modern readers find more sympathetic, are fighting for their city's survival and for their wives and children (15.

494–9); the scenes in Troy in book 6 show us something of what this means. Hence the Trojans, a threatened community, have no choice but to fight. Whether the war is worth fighting, whether the suffering is justified, is something which can only be considered by those on the Achaean side, and in the *Iliad* only Achilles has the leisure and the insight to ask such questions.

At the heart of the value-system of the Homeric heroes is honour, τιμή, expressed through the respect of one's peers and embodied in tangible forms – treasure, gifts, women, an honourable place at the feast. In time of war it is inevitable that honour be won above all through prowess in battle, ability as a leader and a fighter. Other qualities are also admired –ability as a speaker, piety, sound judgement and advice, loyalty, hospitality, gentleness, but these are secondary and the last would indeed be out of place in combat. The crisis of the *Iliad* arises because the greatest of the Greek warriors is not given the honour (both prizes and respect) which he feels to be his due. Because he is a hero, and quick to anger, he will not tolerate this treatment. The situation is worsened by the tactless and injudicious aggressiveness of Agamemnon, and there are no constitutional procedures which can defuse the dispute. It has been plausibly argued that Agamemnon has no clearly defined authority over his fellow-kings, but acts as *de facto* overlord because of the size of his forces (100 ships) and his relationship to the wronged Menelaus.[40] A further contributing factor is Achilles' bitterness at the prospect of a short life: in his knowledge of his own future he differs from all other major characters in the poem (1. 352, 9. 410ff., etc.). Despite his passionate account of his own motives in book 9, his fellow-Greeks cannot understand the depth of his feelings.

The heroic outlook on life, above all as expressed in the speeches of Achilles, is one of the great contributions of the *Iliad* to western literature.[41] Modern discussions have perhaps tended to schematize 'heroic ethics' too rigidly. A few memorable lines are naturally prominent in these discussions: 'always to excel, and to be superior to other men' (6.208 = 11. 784); 'one omen is best, to fight for one's native land' (12. 243); 'I feel terrible shame before the Trojans and the Trojan women with their trailing robes, if like a base man I hang back and skulk away from the war' (6. 441–3). Most famous of all, justly, is Sarpedon's speech to Glaucus in book 12, which sums up the hero's credo with moving simplicity and realism (12. 310–28).

Glaucus, why is it that we two are held in the highest honour in Lycia, with pride of place, the best of the meat, the wine-cup always full, and all look on us like gods, and we have for our own use a great cut of the finest land by the banks of the Xanthos. . . ? That is why we should now be taking our stand at the front of the Lycian lines and facing the sear of battle. . . . Dear friend, if we were going to live for ever, ageless and immortal, if we survived this war, then I would not be fighting in the front ranks myself or urging you into the battle where men win glory. But as it is, whatever we do the fates of death stand over us in a thousand forms, and no mortal can run from them or escape them – so let us go, and either give his triumph to another man, or he to us. (tr. M. Hammond)

Things are not as simple as Sarpedon's account suggests. There is a potential conflict between the striving for individual excellence and the collaborative effort to achieve an end in unison: the individual may pursue his own prestige to the detriment of the army as a whole, as happens when Achilles dismisses his fellow-Greeks and allows them to die.[42] Similarly Hector dreads the accusation, partly justified, that in his pride and self-confidence he has destroyed the host (22. 107). The conflict of interest between personal honour and civic responsibility would remain a key issue in Greek society: in the fifth century, the *Ajax* of Sophocles memorably develops the theme.[43]

The special status of Achilles makes him a special case: a more 'normal' hero, Diomedes for instance, would not react so tempestuously to an insult as Achilles, nor hold out so long against Agamemnon's overtures.[44] Moreover, though all heroes value honour and respond to challenges, different heroes excel in different fields: thus Odysseus is superior at stratagem and counsel, Achilles in combat. Paris, archer and sensualist, seems only to be a hero on a part-time basis, though it is true that he responds readily enough to protests from Hector. Taplin has argued that the whole conception of a 'heroic code' should be abandoned as over-simplifying; in particular, he rejects the assertion by Finley (in one of the weakest sections of a valuable book), that 'The heroic code was complete and unambiguous, so much so that neither the poet nor his characters ever had occasion to debate it.'[45] In this emphatic form such a view is clearly untenable: the characters of the epic regularly hold rational as well as heated discussions of proper conduct, though it is of course true that they do not debate abstractions in the manner of speakers in Plato's dialogues. Patroclus faces a conflict of loyalties, between his friend Achilles and the rest of the Greeks. Nestor, Odysseus, and Diomedes in various scenes recall Agamemnon to the demands of his position and correct his misguided suggestions. In book 19, the argument between Odysseus and Achilles about whether the army should eat is a dispute between passion and expediency. Sound advice and good judgement are valued, and Achilles himself ruefully admits that others are superior to himself in these areas.[46] But it remains true that apart from Achilles few of the heroes in the *Iliad* have cause or opportunity to question the values by which they live or the justification for their own behaviour.

In an influential discussion E. R. Dodds described Homeric society as a 'shame-culture' rather than a 'guilt-culture'; that is, the primary source of morality in that society was what others said and thought about you, rather than a self-conscious assessment of the moral rightness and wrongness of one's actions, irrespective of others' opinions.[47] Homer's heroes are indeed alert to potential loss of face, and this motivates many of the most important decisions of the poems. 'I would be called a coward and a good-for-nothing, if I am to yield to you in whatever you say', declares Achilles to Agamemnon (1. 293–4). 'I feel shame before the Trojans,' says Hector, and remains on the field to face his death (22. 105, echoing 6. 442). Subsequent interpretation has sometimes taken this insight so far as virtually to deny any other moral force in the Homeric universe: Homeric society is, it is claimed, a 'results-culture', where only success counts.[48] Competitive values must overwhelm gentler attitudes and cooperative ethics.[49] Moreover, the inner man – the sense of obligation, responsibility, or conscience – is virtually eradicated. Here moral and psychological analysis meet, since it has also been maintained that 'Homeric man has no unified concept of what we call "soul" or "personality".'[50]

A more moderate version of this argument is now gaining ground. As Dodds himself allowed, shame and guilt are not mutually exclusive motivations, in an individual or a society, and Homer's characters do show themselves affected by other considerations besides loss of face.[51] Indeed, *aidōs* itself, the term commonly rendered as 'shame', is a concept which covers more than the English term might imply: it also embraces embarrassment, a sense of inhibition, and respect, including self-respect.[52] Important passages can be cited in which other moral or emotional factors override the simple consideration of 'what people will say'. Achilles did not strip Andromache's father of his armour, 'for he felt awe at that in his heart' (6. 417 *sebassato*). Achilles' grief and self-reproach at the harm he has brought upon Patroclus (and indeed his other friends) also go beyond any sense of loss of prestige (18. 102–4, 21. 134–5). *Aidōs* is felt towards the suppliant in the case of Priam in book 24, yet many suppliants are slain elsewhere in the poem, and there is no implication that Achilles would have been regarded with disapproval by his peers if he had struck down the aged king. It is not loss of face he fears, but (if anything) the anger of the gods; even that motive is overwhelmed by fellow-feeling and pity for a weak old man.

What of heroic morality in the context of the battlefield?[53] That men die in war is a truism (calculations differ, but one scholar counts 318 deaths in the *Iliad*); but the *way* in which Homer's characters kill, the fervour of bloodlust and the viciousness of some of the wounds, have disturbed many readers in recent times. There is a certain taste for gruesome descriptions, and some of the wounds, though occasionally impossible, are ghoulishly narrated.[54] The spear lodged in a dying man's heart still vibrates in the air with the desperate efforts of the heart's final beating (13. 441–4); a man's eyeballs fall to the earth at his feet (13. 616–7, 16. 741–2); the brain comes oozing out from the eyeholes along the spear (17. 297). Agamemnon, in a scene which sets the pattern for denial of supplications in the poem, urges Menelaus to kill the helpless Adrastus: let no Trojan escape, not even the child still slumbering in the mother's womb (6. 57–60).[55] Dead men are decapitated, their heads sent rolling through the crowd of the battlefield (11. 146, 261, 13. 203). Hector threatens to stick the head of Patroclus upon a stake (17. 126 and 18. 177), and the related threats of denial of burial and permanent mutilation of the corpse gain prominence by increasingly frequent repetition in the last third of the epic.[56] That threat is finally perpetrated by Achilles upon Hector; his revenge for Patroclus also extends to the unique horror of human sacrifice, passed over hastily and perhaps uneasily by the poet.[57] The ultimate barbarity of cannibalism does not go beyond a threat, though uttered with appalling force: 'If only the strength and the heart within me might drive me to hack off your limbs and eat them raw, such harm you have done me.'[58]

How are we to regard these endlessly brutal slayings? Is this the inevitable content of a battle epic, which Homer would avoid if he could? That view would be hard to sustain, given the fullness of the description and the length at which Homer narrates these conflicts. When a hero launches upon an *aristeia*, the audience is surely meant to sympathize with his energy and to relish the excitement of the battlefield, to enjoy the cruel wit of the taunts directed at his opponents; the analogies drawn with the modern western or war film are not unreasonable.[59] It does not follow, however, that Homer is merely a glorious primitive, revelling in the savagery of an age in which violence came naturally.[60] We must distinguish the poet from his characters, and also between the characters in the heat of battle and in calmer or more reflective moments. The violence of the slaughter is balanced by the sympathetic treatments of the victims, whose deaths are often softened with a beautiful simile or dignified with one of the famous epitaphs or 'necrologues'.[61] Besides the similes, the extended description of the scenes on Achilles' shield reminds us of other aspects of life, far from the horrors: there we find scenes of marriage and celebration, ploughing and harvesting, within the framework of earth, sea, and sky. War is on the shield too, but it is a more 'normal', local kind of warfare, seen as a part of the larger world of human existence.[62]

The anger and distress of the survivors in the war, and still more the moving portrayal of the non-combatants such as the women of Troy or Briseis in the Greek camp, make sufficiently clear that dismay at the savagery and grief for those who have fallen are not inappropriate or anachronistic reactions. As for Achilles' mutilation of Hector, it seems important that this is a repeated action, prolonged artificially for days after the actual slaying; in this it differs from the decapitations and other violent wounds perpetrated by Agamemnon and Meriones.[63] The continuous victimization of Hector represents an impossible wish on Achilles' part to extend his revenge indefinitely; it would not even be possible if the gods were not preserving Hector's corpse from decay, and in the scene on Olympus in book 24 we see that the gods themselves, led by Zeus and Apollo, view Achilles' excesses with displeasure. To deny that Homer treats death in war as something pitiful, even tragic, is to deny something vital to the greatness of the *Iliad*.

Gods and men[64]

It is obvious that the gods are fundamental to the nature of the *Iliad*. Not only do their activities underlie the action and provide its premises (the Judgement of Paris, the abduction of Helen), and not only do they regularly intervene in the events narrated in the poem; the poet also allows his audience to observe the life of the gods, which becomes an essential foil to the existence of men. 'Thus the gods have woven destiny for unhappy mortals, for them to live in misery. But they themselves are free of cares.' (24. 525–6) The most important aspect of the gods in the *Iliad* is the way in which they help to define the human condition.

Immortal themselves, the gods are involved in various ways in the world of mortals. They depend on them for sacrifice and regard this and the other honours which humans pay them as their due. Divinities may also be the parents of mortals through brief liaisons with mortals: Aphrodite and Aeneas, Zeus and Sarpedon, and above all Thetis and Achilles: her marriage to Peleus seems to be an unusual case of a longer relationship, but by the time of the *Iliad* she has returned to the sea and Peleus lives alone. Gods may also have particular favourites among mortals, without any kinship between them: Aphrodite cares for Paris, Athena for Odysseus. More broadly, this favouritism extends to cities and their peoples: although the gods receive worship from all, they may have special affection for certain places: thus Hera cares most for Argos, Sparta, and Mycenae, while Zeus admits to particular affection for Troy (4. 44–52). In the *Iliad* the gods are thoroughly involved in the war, often fighting in disguise on one side or the other. Athena, Hera, and Poseidon have a special hatred for Troy: in vain the Trojan women convey rich offerings to Athena's temple in an attempt to win her over (6. 237–311). It is a striking example of Homer's sympathy with the Trojans that they are not represented as worshipping some separate pantheon of barbarian gods (contrast Virgil, *Aeneid* 8. 698 ff.).[65]

As in other areas, we must distinguish between what the characters know of the gods and what the poet tells or represents.[66] The mortals in the Homeric poems generally regard the gods as powerful supporters; in particular, they regularly assume that they will reward piety and uphold justice. Thus in book 4 Agamemnon declares that the Trojans, who have broken the truce, will receive certain punishment as oathbreakers should; similarly Menelaus declares that Paris and the other Trojans will be punished in the end for their offences against Zeus god of hospitality. The reality is more complex and disturbing, for the gods as shown in their own habitat display little concern for justice as humans understand it. Zeus yields to Thetis' importuning out of reluctance to reject her request (and perhaps from gratitude for past favours), even though it will mean the death of many Greeks. The gods themselves plot to disrupt the truce sworn in their name. Apollo strikes Patroclus down and renders him helpless, as later Athena lures Hector to his doom. The favouritism shown by Aphrodite to Paris is even less defensible on moral grounds: having aided him in his seduction of Helen, she whisks him away from deserved retribution. Although gods do sometimes respond to human prayers, their response is swiftest when their own honour is involved, as when Apollo sends plague to punish the Greek army for spurning his priest.[67] The heartfelt prayer of Hector, that his son may grow up to be a great fighter and bring joy to his mother, receives no reply (6. 476–81).[68]

This contrast between human and divine perspective permits much irony and pathos. Human hopes and fears are prompted by their lack of knowledge of the future; even Achilles understands only in part what his own future involves, and is crucially blind to the significance of a divine warning (18. 6–14). Agamemnon is deluded by a false dream, and supposes he will sack Troy on the very next day (2. 35–40). Patroclus asks Achilles to send him forth to battle, 'in his great folly, for he was praying for evil death and doom for himself' (16. 46–7); much is made in book 16 of the fact that Patroclus is fighting, so to speak, on borrowed time. Even when a divine message grants a mortal some insight, it is partial and often misunderstood or neglected: thus Hector forgets the limitations set on his success, and anticipates further victories beyond the day that Zeus promised him (11. 193–4, 17. 453–5, and 18. 293–5).[69] The gods themselves feel the pity of the situation: rather than presenting them solely as capricious or sadistic gamesters, Homer often shows Zeus in particular observing events with concern and compassion (15. 12ff., 16. 644ff., 17. 198–208). Yet the essence of the divine is that it is separate from the human: the gods can always turn away and rest their eyes from combat, which man cannot escape (13. 1–7). For this reason mankind and its concerns can be regarded as trivial: 'you would not call me sensible if I were to fight with you over wretched mortals', comments Apollo to Poseidon (21. 462–4, cf. 1. 574, 8. 428). The exception is Thetis: once married to a mortal, devoted to her mortal son, she is bound up with the human world as the other gods are not.[70]

The paradigm case of the contrast between human and divine spheres is the first book of the *Iliad*, in which the disagreements on Olympus, arising from Hera's suspicion of Zeus, mirror the human quarrel between Achilles and Agamemnon. The uncertain authority of Agamemnon is contrasted with the unchallengeable supremacy of Zeus, king of the gods; the comical figure of Hephaestus, the peace-maker, is a light-hearted reflection of Nestor, who intervenes without success in an effort to calm the heroes. Detailed verbal connections confirm the parallel. But the scene on earth ends with the angry departure of Achilles, which will bring 'innumerable woes'; on Olympus, although bitterness remains, the quarrel is temporarily suspended as the gods laugh at Hephaestus' antics. Forgetting the affairs of mortals, they turn to enjoy the feast and the song of Apollo and the Muses. Human beings cannot be important enough to spoil the festivities. This opposition, between tragically serious mortals and frivolous divinities, is one of the most brilliant creative strokes of the epic tradition. The 'divine comedy' can, however, be overstated: it is always possible for the gods to reassert their authority and their dignity, as Zeus does in this book. Yet total seriousness is denied them, for they are immortal and cannot suffer or perish. Hence Longinus' famous paradox: 'Homer, it seems to me, has done his best to make the men of the Trojan war gods, and the gods men' (*On the sublime* 9.7).

Despite the frequency with which the gods appear and the apparent abundance of detail in their treatment, the *Iliad* is extremely selective in its presentation of the divine. The focus is mainly on a few major divinities (Zeus, Apollo, Hera, Athena, Aphrodite, Poseidon; more rarely Hephaestus, Hermes, Iris, and others). The earlier background of wars against the gods, including the overthrow of Cronos, is taken for granted but only mentioned in vague terms. There are passing references to Demeter, Dionysus, Hades, Persephone, the Erinyes, and other powers, but these do not play speaking roles. The exclusion of Demeter and Dionysus has sometimes been explained on the grounds that they are less aristocratic, more popular gods; it may be more plausible to maintain that they are benefactors of all mankind, and so not easily fitted into the partisan line-up of deities in the Trojan war. The powers of the underworld are more easily explained, since the *Iliad* is clearly averse to this more uncanny side of the supernatural; we hear almost nothing of what Hades' realm is like, and the finality of death is a central fact of the *Iliad*, an essential premiss of the heroic outlook. There are no exceptions: 'even Heracles died', says Achilles as he accepts his own fate; and Castor and Pollux both lie under the soil in their homeland. The *Odyssey*, by contrast, allows Menelaus immortality together with Helen, daughter of Zeus, and seems also to be aware of the legend that Castor and Pollux enjoyed immortality day and day about. Later poetry was still more accommodating.[71]

Those gods who do appear are presented as an extended family, mostly resident together on Olympus; like any family, they have their disagreements and their changing moods. Zeus is affectionate towards both Aphrodite and Athena; Hera uses her feminine charms to try to get her way; Aphrodite is sometimes at odds with Hera, sometimes willing to help her. In other scenes the appropriate human parallel may be rather the court of a king and his fellow-nobles: we have seen that Zeus possesses the authority that Agamemnon would like to have, but he sometimes needs to defend or justify his position, sometimes concedes ground in the face of pressure from below (as at the opening of book 4). In book 15 Poseidon asserts his status like a blustering aristocrat, but eventually yields to the threat of Zeus's superior power (185–217).

Some at least of Homer's conception of the gods is 'poetic' in the sense that it probably lacks any basis in cult. Homeric religion is both selective and creative. The detailed description of scenes on Olympus, such as the cloud-garage in which Hera keeps her chariot; the robots of Hephaestus; Poseidon's chariot ride, with the sea-creatures gambolling in his wake; the mysterious ichor which runs in the gods' veins – all of these are surely colourful elaborations. The idea of a god intervening in human disguise is closer to everyday belief,[72] but the forms which that belief is given in epic spring from a poetic imagination: Athena seizing Achilles by the hair from behind, whereupon he spins round and recognizes her, though for others she is invisible (1. 194–200); Apollo smashing through the Achaean wall like a playful child destroying a sandcastle (15. 360–6); Zeus brandishing the aegis high upon Mt Ida, while thunder shakes the mountain (17. 591 ff.). Images such as these influenced all later Greek poetic presentation of the gods and much of Greek art.[73] The preeminent example is Pheidias' statue of Zeus at Olympia, one of the wonders of the ancient world: the artist is said to have modelled it on the majestic lines in which Zeus nods his head in promise to Thetis (1. 528–30, with Dio Chr. 12. 25, etc.).

I have implicitly assumed that one form of interpretation, which sees the gods as symbols of natural forces or human psychological impulses, is mistaken. Such an approach not only makes nonsense of the scenes in which gods are represented on their own, talking, fighting, or making love; it also runs into difficulties even with the scenes such as Athena's restraint of Achilles, or Helen's exchange with Aphrodite, which the approach was devised to explain. For the purposes of the poem, the gods are real and play a physical part in the poem: they are part of the natural world, though existing on a higher plane than mortals. As we have seen, the poet embroiders their life and personalities imaginatively (unexceptionable, in a society which lacked a formal creed limiting the options of believers); he sometimes introduces characters who are indeed personifications (Fear and Panic, companions of Ares, for example). But to suggest that the gods were fictions or symbols to the poet or his audience is perverse. The precise relationship of divine influence and human response is more difficult: sometimes we seem to have 'double motivation', where the divine prompting duplicates the natural reaction of the mortal character, but in certain cases the god's influence seems more compelling (as perhaps in 16. 684–91). But even then, the gods seem to work on what they find in the human heart: it is predictable, for instance, that the resourceful Odysseus should be the one whom Athena prompts to stop the rout in book 2 (167 ff.).[74] Naturally enough, mortals are often confused or uncertain in these cases; in some circumstances tact or self-defensiveness may cause one of them to emphasize the divine role unjustifiably.[75] But the normal Homeric rule is that a human is responsible for his or her actions, whether or not a god was involved (something which it is hard for the characters to establish). With rare exceptions, there is no suggestion that the presence of the gods eliminates human motivation or decision-making.[76]

The vindictiveness of Hera and Athena, and the frivolity of the gods in combat, astonish readers who assume that gods should be upholders of morality and should exemplify that morality in their own behaviour. Yet although the links are sometimes tenuous, religion is not entirely dissociated from morality in Homer. We have seen that the mortal characters expect that oathbreakers will receive punishment: the invocations at solemn moments of ritual in books 3 and 19 refer to such punitive action as taking place in the underworld, and these assumptions are not contradicted elsewhere in the poem. Zeus is also concerned with oaths, and in certain passages seems to be regarded as lord of hospitality.[77] A difficult passage in book 1 seems to associate the leading Greeks with Zeus in their function as overseers of the *themistes*, 'ordinances' (1. 238–9). In a famous simile Zeus is describes as sending storms upon men who have perverted justice in the assembly (16. 384–93); the vocabulary and morality seem close to the *Odyssey* and to Hesiod's *Works and Days*.[78] Most important of all is book 24, where the gods debate, if not the justice, at least the propriety of Achilles' continued revenge, and where Zeus declares that he must be bought to rein or suffer the gods' anger. Hector's piety, stressed throughout that book, deserves some recognition and reward. In a work which narrates an episode of destructive war, in which good men die on both sides, the gods must often seem callous or malicious. In some episodes they are seen as anxious to save their favourites, but the opposition from other gods is too great (a good example of the explanatory powers of polytheism). In other cases it seems that even the gods, including even Zeus, must yield to the impersonal force of fate: thus Sarpedon must die, and Zeus himself weeps tears of blood for his son.[79] This too is a poetic concept introduced for pathetic effect, and should not be pressed for theology. There is more explicit reflection on the gods' role in relation to human wrongdoing in the *Odyssey* (p. 63 below), though even there the poet does not achieve a totally coherent picture.[80]

Choices and consequences

As has already been implied, Homeric characters are clearly conceived personalities who make deliberate decisions.[81] Often but not always these are based on rational considerations or moral assumptions: thus Odysseus contemplates flight in book 11, but concludes that this is not a step that he, an *aristos*, one of the heroic élite, can legitimately take (11. 403–10).[82] In many cases the character's choice is made in the heat of the moment, sometimes in the grip of anger, grief, hatred, anxiety, or some other highly emotional force. Aristotle compared epic to drama: both genres present individuals in action, and it is through their actions and choices that their character is illuminated.[83] This could be shown in detail by following the presentation of many of the characters, but the most rewarding and important cases are Hector and Achilles. A brief survey of the major choices of each of these two heroes will assist comparison.

   The chief scenes involving Hector in significant decisions are in book 6, where he resists the blandishments of his womenfolk, above all the pleading of his wife, and resolves to return to the battle; in book 18, where he violently rejects the advice of Polydamas to return to the city; and in book 22, where he chooses to remain outside the walls despite the pleas of his father and mother.[84] Later in the same book his nerve cracks and he runs from Achilles, his former resolve shaken; deceived by Athena, he stands and fights after running; finally, seeing his doom clearly, he makes a last heroic stand: 'let me at least not die without effort and without glory, but only once I have achieved some great deed, for posterity to be told of.' (22. 304–5) Each of these scenes has been much discussed: in the first, we see what Hector is fighting for, and what he means to his family, and we witness the transition from bleak realism, as he acknowledges the inevitable fate of Troy, to a tempered hope for the future founded on resolution.[85] In the second, the key example of Hector's bad judgement, we see a more violent and over-confident side of his character.[86] This enthusiasm for battle and assurance of success has been steadily built up by the triumphs of books 11 to 17, in a sense Hector's *aristeia*.[87] The energy of his attack can be seen as fuelling his own arrogance. The ancient scholiasts dealt harshly with Hector's proud declarations, and modern critics are sometimes tempted to speak of *hubris*,[88] but Hector's response is all too human. It is natural and even justifiable for him to be overjoyed by what the Trojans have achieved. His mistake is to forget the limitation set by Zeus and to think himself a match for Achilles. In book 22 he is shown more sympathetically: in a moving soliloquy, he laments his folly in rejecting good advice, flinches at the thought of humiliation, considers and rejects the vain notion of throwing himself on Achilles' mercy, and finally braces himself – though only briefly – to confront his formidable opponent. His introspection, his moment of panic, and his deluded joy at the appearance of Athena/Deiphobus all show his humanity, as a foil to Achilles, who in this episode appears both more and less than human. In general, what emerges from a survey of this kind is that Hector's decisions are both more conventionally heroic and more constrained by external circumstance than the choices of Achilles.[89]

   To illustrate this further requires some general comment on Achilles' situation.[90] Three points are highlighted from the beginning: Achilles is the supreme fighter, 'the best of the Achaeans',[91] far outshining his nominal overlord Agamemnon;[92] he is the son of a goddess, who has access even to the ear of Zeus; and he is to die young. The details of his fate are revealed gradually, and in book 9 he apparently still has some freedom to choose another destiny, but the overwhelming impression is that Achilles is unlikely to accept that inglorious option. In his reply to the embassy he shows himself keenly aware of the progress of the war (esp. 9. 348–55); he makes some concessions in the course of the episode; in book 11 he is still observing the combat from a distance, and it is because he cannot turn his back on the war that he sends Patroclus on his fateful mission to gather news (11. 599–617). Achilles' situation is more complex than Hector's, his personality still more passionate and impulsive. Each of his decisions is important and in its way extraordinary: his initial decision to withdraw from the war; his rejection of the embassy's overtures, contrary to precedent and to the original advice of Athena; his concession in book 16, to send out Patroclus in his place; his determination to avenge Patroclus (this is the natural heroic response, but is made to seem momentous by the link with his own death: 'next after Hector is your death waiting', mourns Thetis); his resolve to pursue revenge even beyond Hector's death, by dragging and exposing his corpse; and finally, his willingness to respect Priam's supplication and release Hector's body for burial. Achilles and Hector are contrasted throughout the poem,[93] not only as the crucial military figures on either side, but in their confrontation of death. Hector, despite the brief moment of realism in book 6, still believes he can win, and only at the very end recognizes that the gods have tricked him: death is inevitable. Achilles, who sought to impose his own will on the gods, finds that his prayers once fulfilled bring him only unhappiness, and accepts death with open eyes (18. 98–9, 22. 365–6 ~ 18. 115–16), without fear though not without bitterness.[94]

Achilles is also a greater hero than Hector, and a more intriguing figure than any of the other heroes, because of his powers as a speaker.[95] This goes beyond formal oratory, of which Odysseus is a master, to a more eloquent style and a broader vision of the world. Recent work has established that Achilles, particularly in major speeches such as those in books 9, 16 and 18, uses a highly individual style which transcends the usual vocabulary, idioms and formulae of Homeric speakers.[96] His speeches are enriched by hyperbolic expressions, exotic place-names, violence which can become tenderness; he also uses similes more abundantly than any other character. These observations reinforce the sense that Achilles is an exceptional hero, not only in his prowess as a warrior but in the extent of his demands, the intensity with which he pursues them, and the magnitude of his self-esteem. The depth of his emotional commitment to Patroclus also seems to go beyond the norms of heroic comradeship, illustrated in more conventional form by the alliance of Idomeneus and

Meriones: notoriously, later Greek readers assumed that the two men were lovers.[97]

The eloquence of the speech in book 9 in which he rejects Odysseus' overtures and expresses his own dilemma has led to a wide range of interpretations. On one view, Achilles is violating the 'heroic code'; on another, he questions its very foundations; or is it that the conventions and assumptions of his world cannot cope with a hero who goes as far as he does?[98] Certainly the embassy, and perhaps even Patroclus himself, find it hard to understand him. Without insisting on an over-rigid definition of 'normal' heroic behaviour, we can at least agree that Achilles sees more clearly and, more important, feels more intensely and expresses himself more powerfully than other characters in the poem. He proclaims his disillusionment with the war and with his destiny, without having an alternative to put in its place. In the superb speech in which he responds to Patroclus' appeal (16.49–100), we see him shift from annoyance to anger, resignation to concession, renewed vindictiveness to sympathetic concern, culminating in the impossible wish that all others should perish, leaving him and Patroclus to sack Troy together: throughout this speech there is the same passionate intensity, but he is no longer certain how he wishes to direct his energy. Once he learns of his friend's death in battle, there is no more room for restraint or indecision, and again his determination to fight, to avenge, and to die is expressed in a series of powerful speeches (esp. 18. 79–93, 98–126, 324–42, 19. 315–37). As in the embassy book, so in the scene in which the hero is 'reconciled' with Agamemnon, it is clear that the other Greek leaders do not fully understand Achilles, who can hardly be restrained from entering battle immediately: they want everything to be as it was before, whereas he is impatient with their talk of gifts and food.[99] Once he has returned to the conflict, the certainty of his own death adds a further note of cruelty to his voice, as most unforgettably in the speech to the ill-fated Lycaon (21. 99–113, cf. 122–35). Although book 9 has been the focus of most discussion of Achilles since the landmark article of Adam Parry, my own inclination would be to attach still more importance to book 24. There, and particularly in the dialogue with Priam, the motifs of impending death and exhaustion with the war recur (540–2), but passion and egotism give way to generosity and resignation, in a sublime expression of the human situation (522–40). The original quarrel had turned Achilles against Agamemnon and all his comrades. His new wrath following the death of Patroclus brought him back to fight against the enemy with far greater fury than before. In the last book of the *Iliad*, he comes to recognize that even an enemy may deserve compassion and respect. This is both heroism and humanity.[100]

NOTES

1. The commentary by Kirk and others (1985–93) is now the first resource; see also Macleod 1982 on book 24, Griffin 1995 on book 9. For general books on the *Iliad* in English see also Bowra 1930, Redfield 1975, Schein 1984 (useful but rather derivative), Mueller 1984, Edwards 1987, Silk 1987 (short but acute), Taplin 1992. In German Reinhardt 1961 and Schadewaldt 1943 are fundamental. Stanley 1993 is extremely useful for book-by-book bibliography even if one finds his analyses over-schematic. More specific studies are mentioned below.

2. 3. 443–6; 3. 204–24; 2. 301–30; for references to earlier campaigning see e.g. 1. 366–9, 6. 414–28, 9. 328–33. For anticipation of the fall of Troy see e.g. 4. 163–5 = 6. 447–9; 15. 69–71; 18. 207 ff., 22. 410–11, etc. For the death of Achilles see below, p. 91. In general see e.g. Kullmann 1960, ch. 5; Griffin 1980, 1; Mueller 1984, 66 f.

3. See esp. K. Reinhardt, 'Das Parisurteil', in *Tradition und Geist* (Göttingen, 1960), 16–36; Griffin 1980, 195 n 49; Richardson 1993, 276–8, a very careful discussion.

4. Taplin 1992, 14–22, with earlier references.

5. G. Nagy, in a series of studies, has described the Homeric epics as 'pan-Hellenic' in a different sense, following use of the term by A. Snodgrass: see e.g. Nagy, *Pindar's Homer* (Johns Hopkins, 1990), 70–1, and the 1995 paper cited in ch. 1 n. 77 above. By this he means that the epic spread widely, and that a common tradition of heroic song was swiftly established throughout the Greek world. It is certainly remarkable that the epic assumes that characters and readers are familiar with place-names and peoples throughout the Greek mainland and islands. This use of 'pan-Hellenism', however, would not affect the point made in my text, that the epic is not obviously nationalistic.

6. As the Meleager-tale especially makes clear (9. 524–99); see also 13. 460, 20. 178 ff., 6. 326 ff.

7. See Page 1959, ch. 6, esp. 248 ff., 286–8; F. M. Combellack, 'Homer and Hector', *AJP* 65 (1944), 209–43. But H. Erbse, 'Ilias und Patroclie', *Hermes* 111 (1983), 1–15 thinks it at least possible that the role of Patroclus has been much expanded.

8. G. Beck, *Die Stellung des 24. Buches der Ilias in der alten Epentradition* (diss. Tübingen, 1964), Macleod 1982, esp. 32–5, Richardson 1993, 1–14. Contrast Seaford 1994, ch. 5 (hardly tenable).

9. In all this discussion it must be borne in mind that the book-divisions are unlikely to be the work of the poet. They are first attested in Alexandrian times, and may well be the work of the school of Aristarchus (Janko 1992, 31; for an earlier date, S. West, *The Ptolemaic Papyri of Homer* (Cologne-Opladen, 1965), 18–25, cf. S. West 1988, 39 f.). Their inadequacy has been strenuously asserted by Taplin 1992, 13, 285–93. It is a major defect of Stanley 1993 that so many of his analyses assume the division goes back to the poet. On the ancient titles given to books or episodes see Stanley 1993, 418 n. 133.

10. 2. 699, 721–6, cf. 686–94. In general on the Catalogue see Kirk's commentary, i. 168–87, 237–40.

11. Ø. Andersen, *Die Diomedesgestalt in der Ilias* (*Symb. Osl.* Suppl. 25, Oslo, 1978) is a detailed study of Diomedes' role. See also Reichel 1994, 217–30.

12. The quotation is from Taplin 1992, 253. See further Redfield 1975, 206–12, Macleod 1982, 28–32.

13. Kakridis 1971, 54–67 rejects simple assertions of Homeric philhellenism; see also Hall 1989, ch. 1. W. M. Sale, 'The Trojans, Statistics, and Milman Parry', *GRBS* 30 (1989), 341–410 argues that Homer greatly expanded the role of the Trojans.

14. 3. 161–80; 24. 762–75, esp. 767, 771–2.

15. Other ways in which Hector and Achilles are contrasted are discussed below, pp. 49–52.

16. Griffin 1980, 3–6 and 23 overstates the case against Paris. On p. 23 he is mistaken in saying that the wound Paris inflicts on Diomedes is 'superficial' (see 19. 48 f.).

17. Macleod 1982, 22 n. 2.

18. See further Schadewaldt 1943, 148; Reinhardt 1961, 63–8; R. J. Rabel, 'Chryses and the opening of the *Iliad*', *AJP* 109 (1988), 473–81. Fenik 1974, 172–207 discusses the *Odyssey*'s fondness for 'character doublets' (e.g. Eurycleia and Eurynome), and illustrates this tendency also from the *Iliad*; cf. Fenik 1968, 148 ff.

19. 5. 318 ff., 792–865. For another case see Patroclus' assault on the wall, 16. 698 ff. (where he yields ground before Apollo) and his renewed onslaught at 783 ff. (where Apollo strikes him down). On the principle see esp. Fenik 1974, 180–7; also M. W. Edwards, 'Topos and transformation in Homer', in Bremer et al. 1987, 50 ff.

20. On retardation in general see M. Reichel, 'Retardationstechniken in der Ilias' ap. W. Kullmann

and M. Reichel (edd.) *Der Übergang von der Mündlichkeit zur Literatur bei den Griechen* (Tübingen, 1990), 125–51; also Bremer ap. Bremer et al. 1987, 33–7. A related technique, misdirection (that is, leading the audience to expect one development and then surprising them) is also present in Homer, though less important: on this see J. M. Morrison, *Homeric Misdirection: False Predictions in the Iliad* (Michigan, 1992).

21. 16. 140–2. See further for explicit cases e.g. 2. 35–40, 419–20, 11. 604, 16. 46–7; for implicit, e.g. 18. 22 ff. (p. 91 below), 18. 207–13 and 219–22, 22. 410–11 (similes which anticipate the sack of Troy). On this whole topic see G. E. Duckworth, *Foreshadowing and Suspense in the Epics of Homer, Apollonius and Vergil* (Princeton, 1933), and now Reichel 1994.

22. E.g. 2. 155, 8. 217, 16. 698 ff.; see further Reinhardt 1961, 107 ff., de Jong 1987, 68–81, H.-G. Nesselrath, *Ungesehenes Geschehen. Beinahe-Episoden im gr. und röm. Epos von Homer bis zur Spätantike* (Stuttgart/Leipzig, 1992).

23. For detailed analysis see Fenik 1968, 217; Janko on 16. 830–63, Richardson on 22. 330–67.

24. 12. 60 ff., 80, 210 ff., 13. 725 ff., 18. 249–313. See Schadewaldt 1943, 104–6; Redfield 1975, 272–7; Bannert 1988, 71–81; Reichel 1994, 175–82.

25. The simile applied to Priam at 24. 480–4 brings out the extraordinary nature of his situation: see Macleod's note.

26. For further analysis of corresponding scenes of this type, see Schadewaldt 1943, Taplin 1992.

27. See further Lord 1960, 68–98; B. B. Powell, *Composition by Theme in the Odyssey* (Meisenheim am Glan, 1977); Edwards 1992, 11–23 (contrast Richardson 1993, 14–24).

28. 1985, ix – though he goes on to allow that 'such dimensions undeniably exist'.

29. I say 'Iliadic' deliberately, since it is not necessarily the case that Homer the man held precisely these views in his everyday life: not only are literature and life distinct, but the *Iliad* itself clearly represents a deliberately selective vision of the heroic world.

30. Morris 1986 and van Wees 1992, 78–89 argue that the epics serve to 'legitimize' kingly rule (similarly Janko 1992, 38). This works well with the Thersites-episode, but surely does not represent the primary purpose of the poems.

31. See further W. G. Thalmann, 'Thersites: Comedy, scapegoat, and heroic ideology in the *Iliad*', *TAPA* 118 (1988), 1–28; S. Halliwell, 'The Uses of Laughter in Greek Culture', *CQ* 41 (1991), 279–96, at p. 282; Reichel 1994, 106 n. 9.

32. Against Page 1959, 315–24, who argued from Thucydides for late interpolation of the passages concerning the wall, see M. L. West, 'The Achaean Wall', *CR* 19 (1969), 255–60 and O. Tsagarakis, 'The Achaean Wall and the Homeric Question', *Hermes* 97 (1969), 129–35.

33. In the Cycle the solution was magical: *Cypria* fr. 20 Allen; cf. Griffin 1977, 40–1.

34. In general on the problems concerning Phoenix see pp. 86 ff. below.

35. Janko ad loc. defends Hector's success in crossing the ditch by appealing to an earlier passage where Apollo opened the way for the Trojan attack (15. 355–8), but the lines still seem difficult.

36. Fundamental treatment by Fenik 1968; cf. also Krischer 1971, Kirk 1976, ch. 3; Latacz 1977, Mueller 1984, ch. 3 (a very useful brief account), Kirk 1990, 15–27. M. M. Willcock, 'Battle Scenes in the *Aeneid*', *PCPS* n.s. 29 (1983), 87–99 compares Homeric and Virgilian battle-scenes.

37. The brief reference to ambushes by Idomeneus in 13. 275–87 (cf. 1. 226 f.) is abnormal. Contrast the *Odyssey*, and see further A. T. Edwards 1985, 18 ff.

38. For another reason for the dropping of this motif see Edwards (see n. 19 above), 57. Edwards 1987, 261 thinks even Sarpedon's uncertainty is a stock motif, cf. 5. 175–6.

39. See Griffin 1980, *passim*, e.g. 48–9.

40. Taplin 1990; Reichel 1994, 198–203.

41. Bowra 1961, ch. 3; cf. his *The Greek Experience* (London, 1957), ch. 2; also the same author's 'The meaning of a heroic age', in Kirk 1964, 22–47.

42. Cf. T. Irwin, *Classical Thought* (Oxford, 1989), ch. 2. Many of the topics covered below are also discussed by C. Gill, *Greek Thought* (*G&R* New Surveys 25, Oxford, 1995), esp. 20–7, 46–9.

43. S. Goldhill, *Reading Greek Tragedy* (Cambridge, 1986), 154–61; note also Aristotle, *Anal. Post.* 97b15, identifying Achilles, Ajax, and Alcibiades as men characterized by pride.

44. Andersen (n. 11 above), Griffin 1980, 74, Macleod 1982, 25 n. 1.

45. Taplin 1992, 6–7, 50–1, 71–2, 166 against Finley 1954 (2nd edn. 1978), 113, cf. 115.

46. See 18. 105–6, and further M. Schofield, '*Euboulia* in the *Iliad*', *CQ* 36 (1986), 6–31; also P. A. L. Greenhalgh, 'Patriotism in the Homeric world', *Historia* 21 (1972), 528–37.

47. Dodds 1951, chh. 1–2, esp. 17–18, 28, 47–50. For modern studies on honour and shame see J. G. Peristiany (ed.), *Honour and Shame: the values of Mediterranean Society* (Chicago, 1965); P. Walcot,

Greek Peasants ancient and modern. A comparison of social and moral values (Manchester, 1970); J. DuBoulay, *Portrait of a Greek Mountain Village* (Oxford, 1974); J. K. Campbell, *Honour, family and patronage: a study of institutions and moral values in a Greek mountain community* (New York, 1964); also H. Lloyd-Jones, 'Honour and shame...' in *Academic Papers* (Oxford, 1990), ii. 253–80 = *A & A* 33 (1987), 1 ff. (German version).

48. Adkins 1960, and many subsequent articles. For criticism see A. A. Long, 'Morals and Values in Homer', *JHS* 90 (1970), 121–39 (contrast Adkins, 'Homeric Values and Homeric Society', *JHS* 91 (1971), 1–14), Lloyd-Jones 1971, ch. 1, Dover 1983, B. Williams, *Shame and Necessity* (Berkeley, 1993), Zanker 1994, esp. ch. 1. C. J. Rowe, 'The Nature of Homeric Morality', in Rubino-Shelmerdine 1983, 248–75, is a review of the issues. N. Yamagata, *Homeric Morality (Mnem.* Suppl. 131, Leiden, 1994) retraces the ground at book length.

49. Again the terminology derives from Adkins, e.g. 1960, 31–46.

50. Dodds 1951, 15. Cf. Snell (Eng. tr. 1953), 17 ff., Fränkel (Eng. tr. 1975), 75 ff. Contrast Williams (n. 48), ch. 1; also Fenik 1978, 68–71, and the works cited in n. 81 below.

51. Lloyd-Jones 1971, 15, 24–7; Dover 1983.

52. D. L. Cairns, *Aidos: the psychology and ethics of Honour and Shame in Ancient Greek Literature* (Oxford, 1993), an exhaustive treatment; see also Williams (n. 48), ch. 4.

53. See further Segal 1971, Vermeule 1979, ch. 3, R. Parker, 'Homer's war music', *Omnibus* 10 (1985), 17–21.

54. The standard instance of an impossible wound is 13. 546 ff. (cf. 442 ff., 616 ff.). For gruesomeness see Griffin 1980, 91, Mueller 1984, 82–6.

55. On supplication see above all J. Gould, '*Hiketeia*', *JHS* 93 (1973), 74–103 (80 n. 39 for a full list); also Thornton 1984, S. Goldhill, 'Supplication and Editorial Comment in the *Iliad*: *Iliad* Z 61–2', *Hermes* 118 (1990), 273–6; K. Crotty, *The poetics of supplication: Homer's Iliad and Odyssey* (Ithaca, London, 1994).

56. Segal 1971, 18–47. See also Griffin 1980, 44–6, for Eastern parallels and contrasts.

57. Threatened at 21. 27 f., fulfilled at 23. 175 f. Cf. G. Murray 1907 (ed. 4, 1934), ch. 5.

58. Achilles to Hector, 22. 346–7; cf. 4. 34–6, Zeus to Hera on her hatred for the Trojans; also 24. 212–13, Hecuba on Achilles. See Redfield 1975, 197–9; Griffin 1980, 20.

59. See Vermeule 1979, esp. 99–103; W. Parks, *Verbal Dueling in Heroic Narrative: the Homeric and Old English Traditions* (Princeton, 1990).

60. A memorable essay by S. Weil, 'The *Iliad* as a poem of force' (originally 1953; Eng. tr. in *Intimations of Christianity among the ancient Greeks* (London, 1957), 24–55) emphasizes both the pity and the horror of Homeric warfare; the horror is more cheerfully accepted by Finley 1954 (2nd edn., 1978), 118, 'The poet and his audience lingered lovingly over every act of slaughter', and by Vermeule 1979, 84, 85, 96, 99, 114 (who speaks of 'wit' and 'ballet' in the battle-scenes).

61. E.g. 4. 473–89 (well discussed by Schein 1984, 73–6), 5. 152–8 (the bereaved father), 11. 241–7 (the bride left behind); more examples in Griffin 1980, ch. 4. For similes used to enhance the pathos of death see e.g. 8. 306–7; D. H. Porter, 'Violent juxtaposition in the similes of the *Iliad*', *CJ* 68 (1972), 11–21.

62. On the shield see Schadewaldt 1944 (4th edn., 1965), 352–74; Reinhardt 1961, 401–11; O. Taplin, 'The shield of Achilles within the *Iliad*', *G&R* 27 (1980), 1–21. There has been much interest in the shield more recently among students of *ecphrasis* (the formal description of a work of art in literature); see now A. S. Becker, *The Shield of Achilles and the Poetics of Ekphrasis* (Maryland and London, 1995), with earlier bibl.

63. It is misguided to lay too much stress on the phrases 'unseemly acts' and 'harsh deeds' (22. 395, 23. 24, 176), used to describe Achilles' actions (as is done by e.g. Bowra 1930, 21, Segal 1971, 13); these phrases do not necessarily convey moral criticisms. See Griffin 1980, 85; Vermeule 1979, 234 n. 11; Hainsworth 1993, 49–50, Richardson 1993 ad loc.

64. See esp. Griffin 1980, chh. 5–6; Erbse 1986; Edwards 1987, ch. 17; Kirk 1990, 1–14; Janko 1992, 1–7. On religion more generally see above all W. Burkert, *Greek Religion* (Oxford, 1985), and J. N. Bremmer, *Greek Religion* (*G&R* New Surveys 24, Oxford, 1994). For illustrations of the gods in art see E. Simon, *Die Götter der Griechen* (Munich, 1969; 3rd edn., 1985).

65. Hall 1989, 43–5.

66. O. Jörgensen, 'Die Götter in ι-μ der Odyssee', *Hermes* 39 (1904), 357–82.

67. Cf. the stories of Niobe (24. 602–9) and of Meleager's father (9. 533–7); cf. Page 1973, 79–83; L. Weiler, *Der Agon in Mythos* (Darmstadt, 1974).

68. On this case, and on prayers in Homer more generally, see Macleod 1982, 42; more bibl. in Reichel 1994, 73.

69. Rutherford 1982, 156–7, with other examples.

70. In general on Thetis' role in the *Iliad* see Slatkin 1991.

71. 18. 117; 3. 243–4; iv. 561 ff.; cf. xi. 299–304, on Castor and Pollux. See M. L. West on Hesiod, *WD* 166–7; Griffin 1977, 42.

72. Cf. xvii. 483–7; E. Kearns, 'The Return of Odysseus: a Homeric Theoxeny', *CQ* 32 (1982), 2–8; R. Lane Fox, *Pagans and Christians* (Harmondsworth, 1986), ch. 4.

73. Burkert (n. 64), 119–25.

74. See esp. Lesky 1961; also M. M. Willcock, 'Aspects of the gods of the *Iliad*', *BICS* 17 (1970), 1–10 = Wright 1978, 58–69.

75. As 3. 164, Priam to Helen; 19. 86 ff., Agamemnon's apology; more outrageously, Paris at 3. 439 (p. 85 below). See Dodds 1951, ch. 1; Hutchinson on Aesch. *Seven* 4–9; Taplin 1990, 75–7, and Edwards 1991, 245 ff. on 19. 85–138.

76. For one particularly complex case, Aphrodite and Helen in *Iliad* 3, see p. 83 below. Another in which psychic intervention is clearly involved, and which seems to involve some distortion of the mortal's 'natural' reactions, is Athena's prompting of Penelope to show herself to the suitors in *Odyssey* xviii, a controversial scene (see Rutherford 1992, 29–33).

77. Zeus invoked at oath-taking, 3. 104, 276, 298 ff., 320. See 3. 351–4 and 13. 625 (Menelaus) for Zeus Xeinios. The oath-breaker Pandarus is indeed killed shortly after his offence, though it is not clear whether this is to be seen as either divine or poetic justice: see A. Parry in M. Parry 1971, lvii n. 1; Taplin 1992, 104–9.

78. Cf. 18. 507–8; Hes. *Th.* 85–6 with West's n.; *WD* 35 f., 250–69.

79. 16. 458–61. In general, W. C. Greene, *Moira: Fate, Good and Evil in Greek Thought* (Harvard, 1944), B. C. Dietrich, *Death, fate and the gods* (London, 1965), Burkert (n. 64), 129–30, Janko 1992, 4–7.

80. W. Jaeger, 'Solons Eunomia', *SPAW* (1926), xi 69–85 = *Scripta Minora* i (Rome, 1960), 315–35 = *Five Essays* (Montreal, 1966), 77–99, at 83 ff.; Dodds 1951, 32–4, Lloyd-Jones 1971, 28–32, Fenik 1974, 208–30, Kullmann 1985.

81. R. Sharples, '"But why has my heart spoken with me thus?" Homeric decision-making', *G&R* 30 (1983), 1–7; S. Halliwell, 'Traditional Greek Conceptions of Character', in Pelling 1990, 32–59; R. Gaskin, 'Do Homeric heroes make real decisions?' *CQ* 40 (1990), 1–15.

82. These and parallel speeches are discussed by B. Fenik, 'Stylisation and Variety: four monologues in the *Iliad*', in Fenik 1978, 68–90, and by G. Petersmann, 'Die Entscheidungsmonologe in den Homerischen Epen', *GB* 2 (1974), 147–69.

83. For bibliography on the relationship of Homer to tragedy see Reichel 1994, 11; ancient texts on the subject are gathered by Herington 1985, 213–15. Some of the connections are discussed in Rutherford 1982, but I would now lay less emphasis on the Aristotelian concept of tragic error (*hamartia*). Seaford 1994, 275–8, 338–44 stresses the differences between the genres.

84. On Hector see esp. Redfield 1975, 109 ff.; also H. Erbse, 'Hektor in der Ilias', in *Kyklos* (Fest. R. Keydell, Berlin, 1978), 1–19 = *Ausgew. Schriften* (Berlin, 1979), 1–18; Reichel 1994, 156 n. 1 (bibl.).

85. See further D. Lohmann, *Die Andromache-Szenen in der Ilias* (Hildesheim, 1988).

86. The point is emphasized not only by the earlier series of exchanges with Polydamas, but also by the carefully planned contrast between this scene and the corresponding Trojan assembly in book 8 (note esp. 8. 542 = 18. 310). Cf. Rutherford 1985, 135.

87. There are of course set-backs, notably the episode in which Hector is wounded (14. 402–522, 15. 262 ff.), but this does not affect the overall pattern.

88. For the scholia see Richardson 1980, 273–4. Moderns who use the term *hubris* (a word remarkably rare in the *Iliad*) are listed and criticized by N. R. E. Fisher, *Hubris. A study in the values of honour and shame in ancient Greece* (Warminster, 1992), 177–8 (now the definitive treatment of this difficult term).

89. See also Schadewaldt 1944 (4th edn., 1965), 268–351.

90. On Achilles generally see the very full bibliography in Reichel 1994, 99 n. 1; also Zanker 1994.

91. Much rhetorical play is made with this phrase: see 1. 91, 244, 412, 2. 82, 16. 271 f., 23. 891, etc.

92. This formulation can stand, even if the case for informality of command structure pressed by Taplin 1990 is accepted in full.

93. See further my remarks in 1982, 157–8, and context.

94. Schadewaldt 1944 (rev. 1965), 234–67; Griffin 1980, 163–4.

95. On Homeric rhetoric see Lohmann 1970, J. Latacz, 'Zur Forschungsarbeit an den direkten Reden bei Homer', *Gräzer Beiträge* 2 (1974), 395–422, Rutherford 1992, 58–69.

96. The essential discussion is by Griffin 1986, developed in 1995; some criticism in Kirk 1990, 28–35. See also Lohmann 1970, esp. 236–45 on book 9; Martin 1989, important though vulnerable in some details.

97. Aeschylus' *Myrmidons* seems to have been particularly important, see frr. 134–7 Radt; also K. J. Dover, *Greek Homosexuality* (London, 1978), 196–201, D. M. Halperin, *One Hundred Years of Homosexuality* (London, 1990), 75–87; Edwards on 18. 82. Homer avoids any suggestion of homosexuality: even the favour shown by Zeus to Ganymede is treated in asexual terms in the *Iliad*, despite reference to the young man's beauty (5. 266, 20. 232–5).

98. A. Parry, 'The language of Achilles', *TAPA* 87 (1956), 1–7 = Kirk 1964, 48–54 = Parry 1989, 1–7, was seminal in this discussion; for specific criticism see M. D. Reeve, 'The language of Achilles' *CQ* 23 (1973),193–5, Lynn-George 1988, ch. 2 (esp. 93–101); and for development see e.g. Redfield 1975, 3–23, 103–6, Edwards 1987, 231–6, Martin 1989, ch. 4; Gill (n. 42 above), 46–7.

99. Edwards' commentary is invaluable on book 19, which earlier treatments often underrated; also valuable is Taplin 1992, 203–18. On the importance of feasting together see Griffin 1980, 14–21, an excellent section.

100. For a different approach see Seaford 1994, 159–80, who lays much emphasis on the importance of ritual in re-integrating Achilles into the community.

III. THE *ODYSSEY*[1]

Must a sequel be inferior?[2]

Although it is theoretically possible (and has been asserted) that the *Iliad* followed the *Odyssey*, or that the two poems were composed quite independently, with no influence from one to the other,[3] majority opinion ancient and modern puts the *Odyssey* later, and assumes it to be in important respects a successor, even a sequel, to the *Iliad*. This position can be maintained in various forms: those who believe in a single master-poet as the creator of both epics may assign the *Iliad* to Homer's youth, the *Odyssey* to his riper years (a position memorably expressed by Longinus); those who follow the ancient separatists can regard the *Odyssey* as a rival work, composed by a poet who immensely admired the *Iliad* but whose own poetic and moral concerns lay elsewhere. On the whole the latter view is now more common, though there are eminent advocates on both sides. In fact it is probably impossible, in a tradition which involved so much use of conventional themes and formulaic material, to decide firmly in favour of common or separate authorship. Whichever view one prefers, the important point seems to be that the *Odyssey* is later, and that it is conceived as a poem on the same scale as the *Iliad*, but differing strikingly in content and ethos.

Some of the arguments for that conclusion are based on detailed allusion and apparent verbal reminiscences, which cannot be reviewed here, and which some scholars, doubtful of the possibility of allusion in an oral poetic tradition, would not accept. More substantial points include the following. (1) The scale of the epics seems to mark them out as unusual in the early period; the Cyclic poems, to judge by the figures that have come down to us, were much shorter. (2) The *Odyssey* adopts a similar technique to the *Iliad* in selecting a limited period from a much longer tale, while using digressions, recapitulation, and prophecy to bring more of that tale within its scope. Most obviously, Odysseus narrates his previous wanderings to the Phaeacians; also, Nestor, Menelaus, and Helen recount some of the hero's earlier exploits. (3) The *Odyssey* looks like a sequel, in that many of the cast of characters of the *Iliad* reappear and act in characteristic fashion: Achilles is disillusioned and bitter, Nestor garrulous, Helen enchanting yet rather enigmatic. Moreover, a very efficient job is done of filling in the background, giving the audience at least in summary form some account of

the events since the close of the *Iliad*. (4) A number of parallels in theme
and structure can be detected: in particular, the culmination in the hero's
long-delayed but bloodthirsty revenge against his enemy (Hector, the
suitors), followed by scenes involving gentler emotions and resolution of
tensions (in the *Iliad* the funeral games and the encounter with Priam; in
the *Odyssey* the reunion with Penelope, and perhaps the coming of peace
in Ithaca).[4] Other parallels which have been suggested include: (a) the
absence of the hero from his proper sphere, and the difficulties this causes
for his comrades or family. (b) the hero's rejection of an easier option,
choosing instead a life which will fulfil his human potential (Achilles in the
end rejects a long but inglorious life; Odysseus rejects immortality with
Calypso); (c) the importance of family ties, and especially the father–son
relationship, in both epics.

The relationship of the *Iliad* and the *Odyssey* can also be seen as an
opposition. The former is a poem of warfare and death, the latter describes
the aftermath of that war, and presents a society in peacetime, though disrupted by abnormal circumstances. The scene of the *Iliad* is deliberately
restricted; the *Odyssey* is a poem of wide horizons (i. 3, 'many were the
cities of men that he saw, and he learned their minds'). The *Iliad* ends
tragically, with the threat of death hanging over both Achilles and the
people of Priam; in the *Odyssey*, the prospects are brighter, with the
reunion of husband and wife and the restoration of order to the community
of Ithaca. Above all, there is a strong contrast between the heroes of the
two epics. On the one hand, the youthful, outspoken, quick-tempered, and
glory-hungry Achilles, the supreme fighter; on the other, the older, cannier
Odysseus, devious and subtle, skilled orator and cunning trickster. Many of
the differences between the poems arise from the nature of the heroes. It is
interesting that already in the *Iliad* they are seen as potential opposites,
even antagonists (note esp. 9. 312–3).[5]

There is a tendency, already evident in ancient criticism, to devalue the
Odyssey in comparison with the *Iliad*.[6] Socrates in Plato refers to this kind
of judgement: 'I have heard your father say that the *Iliad* is a finer poem
than the *Odyssey* by as much as Achilles is a better man than Odysseus'
(*Hipp. Min.* 363b). Longinus notoriously thought it showed signs of an old
man's weakening powers (9. 13–15). But given the differences already
described, it should be clear that it is dangerous to judge the two poems by
the same criteria. If the *Odyssey* follows on from the *Iliad* while also seeking to achieve something different, if indeed it represents a challenge or a
transformation of Iliadic themes, then differences are what we would
expect. We do not criticize a comedy because it does not live up to the

criteria required of a tragedy. Happily, recent criticism has been much more sensitive to the special qualities of the *Odyssey* – its subtlety of characterization, the skill with which narrative situations are developed, the extensive use of irony and double-meanings. The fascination of the travel books, full of magic, monsters, and mystery, has always captured the imagination. The *Odyssey* combines what we may call folk-tales (not only scenes such as the adventures with a one-eyed giant, but the disguise of Odysseus and the test of the bow) with heroic mythology, and integrates both within a firm and explicit moral framework. The combination is more elaborate than that of the *Iliad*, where the fixed setting and wartime conditions impose a greater uniformity. Given the very different task which the poet of the *Odyssey* was undertaking, it is remarkable that the poem presents the reader with such a coherent picture of an imagined world.

In some ways the *Odyssey* is a more self-consciously 'literary' poem than the *Iliad*.[7] Although the *Iliad* includes invocations of the Muse, Helen's weaving (a figure for the artist at work?), Achilles' solitary singing of the 'glorious deeds of men', and the magnificent description of the shield, the *Odyssey* goes further, including poets among the cast of characters (Phemius in Ithaca, Demodocus at Alcinous' court). In the final book, Agamemnon's ghost remarks that the virtue of Penelope will be acclaimed through the ages, while the treacherous Clytemnestra will be remembered with ignominy. This passage comes very close to self-reference (xxiv. 196–202). Moreover, there is story-telling elsewhere, as the heroes reminisce about the Trojan war or recount their experiences to the admiring Telemachus.[8] Odysseus himself is on several occasions compared to a bard (xvii. 518–21, xxi. 404–9), and once a comparison of this kind includes a reference to the lying tales of strangers (xi. 364–9); although this is used as a contrast with Odysseus' narrative, it is a two-edged comment, since we see the hero spinning fictitious tales about himself with equal fluency.[9] Some ancient readers even seem to have taken the 'authentic' travel-narrative, with which Odysseus entertains the Phaeacians, as another lying tale invented by the hero himself,[10] though Homer gives us no justification for this.[11]

More specifically, the songs of Demodocus described in book 8 can be read as each contributing to an allusive commentary on the *Iliad*.[12] The first song refers to a quarrel between two Greek heroes, Achilles and Odysseus, at which Agamemnon rejoices (viii. 72–82). He reacts in this unexpected way, it seems, because he sees their quarrel as fulfilling a prophecy; but in fact the prophecy referred to his own much deadlier conflict with Achilles, still in the future. The motifs of Agamemnon's error,

delusive prophecy, and the will of Zeus, all recall important themes of the
Iliad. The second song describes the love-affair of Ares and Aphrodite and
Hephaestus' successful trapping of the adulterous pair: Hephaestus pre-
tends to go away on a journey, but lays a snare and returns to find Ares and
Aphrodite naked and entrammelled (266–366). The sensuous, immoral
behaviour of the gods reminds us of the love-scene of Zeus and Hera on Ida
(14. 292–353), and more generally of the conduct of the gods in the *Iliad*.
Moreover, looking beyond the song itself, we can see analogies between the
plotting Hephaestus, who deceives others and unexpectedly returns, and
the role of Odysseus later in the poem. Yet the contrast between divine and
human worlds is equally important. Aphrodite is no Penelope, and the
immortal Ares cannot be punished by death, but only by ineffectual bar-
gains over compensation.[13] The third song of Demodocus (499–520)
describes the sack of Troy, so often anticipated in the last part of the *Iliad*.
Here Odysseus breaks down and weeps over the past: the simile which
describes his reaction compares him to a wife bereaved of her husband and
dragged away by callous soldiers. This passage reminds us of the sympathetic treatment in the *Iliad* of the women of Troy, above all the
widowed Andromache, and of the cruelty that accompanies the sack of a
city. All of these scenes play a part in the overall movement of the
Phaeacian episode, which helps restore the storm-tossed hero to his full
heroic stature;[14] but they also suggest new perspectives from which to
regard the world of the *Iliad*.[15]

Themes, structure, ethos

The construction of the *Odyssey* illuminates the character and general
interpretation of the poem. Firstly, there is the delay in introducing the
hero. Whereas Achilles was named in the first line of the *Iliad*, was
described as summoning the assembly at line 54, and dominated much of
the first book, in the proem to the *Odyssey* the hero is not named[16] but only
periphrastically described; he does not appear until well into book v. Before
that we are introduced to most of the other principal characters of the
poem, and hear much about the hero's past prowess; the scenes in Ithaca
also make clear the urgent need for his return.

Secondly, the poem falls easily into two halves, the first half ending at
xiii. 92, where the Phaeacian ship speeds across the waves towards Ithaca,
carrying the sleeping Odysseus: he is there described in lines which seem to
echo the proem of book i. At this point we move from sea-going adventures
to land; the wanderings are coming to an end, and the remainder of the

poem will be principally concerned with the kingdom of Ithaca. The poet is consciously marking the half-way point of his tale. In particular, there are numerous points in which Odysseus' arrival and experiences in Phaeacia anticipate and prepare for the homecoming to Ithaca.[17]

Thirdly, the poem's narrative technique is throughout more complex than that of the *Iliad*, especially as regards scene-changing.[18] The poet has constructed parallel narratives, supposedly beginning at the same point: Athena is sent to Ithaca to despatch Telemachus on his travels in search of his father, and Hermes is to be sent to Calypso's isle, to instruct the nymph to launch Odysseus on his journey home. In fact the second part of the proposed plan seems to be delayed, and a further divine exchange is required in book v before Hermes sets off. Later, there is a similar blurring of the time-scale when Odysseus is back in Ithaca and Athena needs to bring Telemachus home from Sparta.[19] The poet is attempting something more elaborate than we find in the *Iliad*,[20] involving the simultaneous development of events on two fronts; indeed, the return of the narrative to Ithaca during Telemachus' absence introduces a third (iv. 624–847). Here as in the lengthy narratives of past events a technique which can be found on a smaller scale in the earlier epic is extended so ambitiously as to alter its nature.

The first four books of the *Odyssey* are conventionally known as the 'Telemachy', a title which highlights the special role of Odysseus' son in the poem.[21] In essence, Athena stirs him from his inertia, forces him to confront the real danger of his situation, and sends him to Pylos and Sparta not because he will find his father there (though he does learn of his present situation), but to 'win glory' and learn from his father's peers. The ancient description of the Telemachy as the 'education' of Telemachus is suggestive, though not universally accepted.[22] By the time Odysseus is back in Ithaca, Telemachus is behaving as a king's son and heir should do, and will be a worthy ally in the final crisis; at the contest of the bow, he shows himself his father's true son by being *about* to bend the bow successfully, but then holding himself back. The Odyssean qualities of self-discipline and concealment are transferred to Telemachus.

From another viewpoint, the wanderings of Telemachus make it possible for the poet to introduce some of the heroes of the Trojan war, and to show their present situation: Nestor secure and prosperous, though still grieving for his son Antilochus, who died saving his father's life; Menelaus also settled in his kingdom, but still saddened by the loss of so many comrades in the war, and enjoying a somewhat ambiguous and puzzling relationship with the still-beautiful Helen. Although Odysseus is still missing, and his household increasingly fear that he must be dead, we anticipate that he will return at last, later than all the other heroes, and win a greater victory, a more successful homecoming, than any of the others. Here the comparison between Odysseus' household and that of Agamemnon is particularly important.[23] Agamemnon returned openly, and his rash confidence laid him open to the assassin Aegisthus; his queen was unfaithful, seduced by her lover during his long absence; his son Orestes has had to take revenge. The disastrous history of Agamemnon shows what might have happened in Ithaca, if Odysseus were less prudent and Penelope less faithful.[24]

The punishment of Aegisthus, mentioned in the first divine scene of the poem, sets the moral tone for the epic. In this poem the gods oversee human morality more consistently and austerely than in the *Iliad*. In general, the Olympians seem more remote from the activities of mankind: there are few scenes in which Zeus and the other gods hold counsel, and several deities prominent in the *Iliad* never appear (especially Hera, Apollo, and less surprisingly Thetis; Aphrodite appears only in Demodocus' song). The main plot really requires only Athena, Odysseus' constant supporter,[25] Poseidon, his persecutor, and Zeus, who arbitrates between them. Other deities such as Hermes occasionally figure, but the general effect is very different. The Trojan war was a major event which aroused the passionate partisanship of many divinities; Odysseus, a single hero though a pious man, is of little concern to the gods other than his patroness. Nevertheless, the gods are of central importance in that the *Odyssey* shows us a world governed by an ethical code which the gods endorse. Wrongdoing will be punished, callous and impious deeds do not prosper. Zeus watches over beggars, suppliants, and others in distress; those who mistreat a guest under their roof can expect to suffer for it. These moral principles are commonly cited by the characters, and in one of the most striking speeches of the poem, Odysseus draws the moral from his success over the suitors, though forbidding the nurse to cry aloud in exultation over the dead. 'It is not holy to crow over dead men. These men were destroyed by the gods' dispensation and by their own wicked deeds, for they honoured none of the men on the earth, neither bad nor good, who came amongst them. So it is that they have met an ugly end through their own rash folly.' (xxii. 412–16)[26] Here Odysseus speaks as an instrument of divine retribution, rather than as a vengeful hero reclaiming his own property from upstarts. It has been claimed that passages like this show the *Odyssey* to be the product of a more advanced ethical or religious outlook than the *Iliad*, but these arguments must be viewed with caution.[27] The poet of the *Iliad* knows about gods concerned with justice (see p. 49), and the *Odyssey* shows a strongly Iliadic divinity in Poseidon, fierce in anger and conscious of his own status. Moreover, although Athena praises Odysseus before Zeus for his piety, she herself loves him for his lies and his deviousness (i. 60–2 versus xiii. 291–9 and 330–8).[28] The different emphasis in the *Odyssey*'s presentation of the gods may well result from the different type of story that the later poem has to tell. Both poems use the gods selectively and appropriately.

But the Olympian gods do not exhaust the supernatural elements of the poem. The *Odyssey* includes cannibal monsters, the bag of winds, the mysterious lotus-fruit with its amnesiac effects, the Cyclops, the cattle of the sun, and a visit to the Underworld.[29] Most of these magical or monstrous features occur in the narrative of Odysseus, which we have already seen to be less realistic than the other parts of the *Odyssey*. It is also important that they take place far away, beyond the familiar geography of the Greek mainland and Ionia: Odysseus leaves the known world behind as early as ix. 80, and attempts to trace his wanderings on the map are inevitably doomed to failure.[30]

Given that the Telemachy and the Ithacan narrative are rooted more deeply in heroic society, it is natural to ask how successfully the poet has integrated the more magical adventures with the rest of Odysseus' experience. Perhaps the most striking point is the way in which this very difference of tone is exploited: Odysseus is presented as a man who must gradually learn to cope with unfamiliar challenges, which conventional heroic behaviour cannot overcome.[31] The claim to be conqueror of Troy cuts little ice with the Cyclops, and to kill the monster while he lies slumbering would be fatal, since Odysseus and his men have not the strength to shift the stone blocking the cave's mouth. Later, open defiance is useless against the immortal Scylla. Odysseus, the untypical hero, must use his wits and cunning; he has the adaptability to deal with these otherworldly horrors. Amongst other things, he learns to conceal his identity, to observe and wait before risking self-exposure. The trick with the pseudonym 'No-man' is the first instance, but this clever stroke is thrown away when Odysseus reveals his identity to the Cyclops once safely out of the cave. In the second half of the poem he will further cultivate anonymity and false identities.

The eleventh book illuminates Odysseus' character and the meaning of the poem through the encounter with Odysseus' past. Homer uses the supernatural setting of the underworld for other purposes besides the ostensible motive of seeking directions from Tiresias. Besides the moving exchange between the hero and his dead mother, a memorable scene

introduces the ghosts of three heroes who perished at Troy or after returning from the war –Agamemnon, Achilles, and Ajax.[32] In ways none the less
important for being implicit, these three men are contrasted with the living
Odysseus, the survivor, who will go on to find his way home and reclaim
wife, family, and kingdom. Particularly effective in this episode is the dialogue with Achilles: nowhere else in Homer is the contrast between their
characters clearer, and yet here Achilles has moved closer to the viewpoint
of Odysseus, for whom heroic achievement is not the only precious thing in
life. For all the disillusionment expressed in book 24 of the *Iliad*, Achilles'
bitterness at his present state sounds a note of realism unheard in the
earlier poem.[33] Book xi is also of great importance in that it makes clear,
through Tiresias' prophecy, that Odysseus' wanderings will not be ended
when he reaches Ithaca: he has 'immeasurable toil, long and hard', still to
come (xxiii. 248–50, cf. xi. 119–37). The end of the *Odyssey* does not leave
the couple to live 'happily ever after'.[34]

Another aspect of the wanderings may be described in cultural or
anthropological terms.[35] The different beings and communities among
whom Odysseus finds himself are characterized by strange practices and
behaviour in comparison with 'normal' human society. The Laestrygonians do not farm (x. 98); Calypso's island is wooded, and has a vine, but
is not cultivated (v. 63–74). The lotus-eaters do not have to farm or work,
they do not cook or eat bread, only the lotus-flower; the food they offer
Odysseus' companions deprives them of an essential aspect of their
humanity, memory (ix. 84, 94–7). The Cyclopes, as Odysseus explicitly
comments, have no assembly-place or laws and do not combine as a community (ix. 112, with context). In Polyphemus' cave other divergences from
human social and ethical codes become manifest. Instead of feeding his
guests, he eats them, and his offer of a 'guest-gift' is a grotesque parody of
the institution: he will eat Odysseus last. Odysseus' wanderings are not just
a series of randomly combined adventures, but are subordinate to an overall conception, whether fully articulated or not, of the nature of human life;
through his encounters with superhuman and subhuman creatures and
their *mores*, Odysseus defines the limits and nature of the human condition.
On this argument it is appropriate that the Phaeacians should represent his
final port of call before his homecoming. They are human, but not wholly
of our world: isolated from mankind, they enjoy an existence close to the
gods, and sail magical ships. But in other respects they seem less than fully
human, for their society is protected from war and they enjoy a carefree,
hedonistic existence.[36]

But the folk-tale element is not confined to books ix–xii. The themes of the wanderer's return and the woman perpetually weaving are both found in folklore; the contest of the bow has been paralleled in Indian epic.[37] As for the supernatural aspect, Menelaus in book iv describes how near Egypt he was obliged to ambush and capture the shape-changing prophet, Proteus; again, the remote and exotic setting makes this kind of tale more acceptable. Even in Ithaca Odysseus is magically transformed by Athena ('I shall make you unrecognizable to all men', xiii. 397), though the nature and degree of his transformation remain ambiguous.[38] This seems to be an example of a general tendency in the *Odyssey*: comparison with parallel folk-tales suggests that Homer has somewhat reduced or underplayed the magical aspects, in order to preserve the sense that this is above all a human drama. Thus in book x the magical plant *moly*, introduced as a protective charm against Circe's enchantment, is forgotten after Odysseus has received it from Hermes, and it is Odysseus' own strength of will that frustrates Circe (x. 327, 329).[39]

   Some reference has already been made to the importance of disguise and concealment,[40] and many of the *Odyssey*'s most striking episodes depend on a contrast between appearance and actuality. This has two major aspects, the failure to recognize a stranger or new arrival, and the concealment or suppression of one's true feelings, whether out of caution or to delay a moment of emotional outpouring. The first book already uses this technique: Athena comes to visit Telemachus, in disguise as a mortal trader; only gradually does she reveal some (false) information about herself; only on her miraculous departure does he realize that she must be a divinity. Thereafter he must conceal this insight and her advice, and give nothing away to the suitors about his plans and new hopes. The poet is fascinated by the notion of the unrecognized stranger, the disguised guest whose identity is relevant, even crucial to the conversation going on around him. This typical Odyssean situation is used with Telemachus at Sparta, with Odysseus in Alcinous' court, in the hut of the swineherd, and above all in his own palace. Multiple ironies result: while Athena in disguise talks with Telemachus of his father's return, Phemius has been singing to the suitors of the homecoming of the Greeks from Troy, and of the part Athena played in that voyage. In the palace of Menelaus, the subject of Odysseus comes up even before Telemachus has been identified as the hero's son, and the young man is overcome by emotion: recognition soon follows. While Odysseus sits unrecognized in the halls of the Phaeacians, the minstrel sings of the quarrel between Achilles and Odysseus. In Eumaeus' hut, he hears talk of himself and his estates. Delayed recognition and ironic double-meanings are typical of the

Odyssey, and especially of its second half, once Odysseus is back among his own people.

Other aspects of these scenes are of equal interest. We see a king in beggar's clothes, kindly treated by poorer folk but spurned and mocked by the aristocrats of the kingdom, who should respect him. The sympathetic treatment of humbler and less heroic characters is another area in which the *Odyssey* offers something new and different from the *Iliad* (though it is true that common people and their lives do figure in similes and on Achilles' shield). The disguised Odysseus is also in a position of unsuspected superiority over those around him: he can question and test them, sounding them out about their feelings towards himself and the prospect of his return. This testing procedure is applied not only to Eumaeus and the suitors, but to Penelope herself. It is in the scenes with her (as earlier before he reveals himself to Telemachus) that he must work hardest to govern his own feelings.

With these words he kissed his son, and shed a tear that fell down his cheeks and to the ground; until that moment he had held the tear back always. (xvi. 190–1)

As for Odysseus, his heart went out to his weeping wife, but beneath his eyelids his eyes kept as firm as horn or iron; he still dissembled, and showed no tears. (xix. 209–12)

Once Odysseus has identified himself to Telemachus, the young man must also show the same self-control, and avoid any outbursts of rage at the way the suitors treat his father. The fidelity and caution of Penelope, who will hardly believe that her husband is really home even after the slaughter, show that she too has the self-discipline appropriate to the wife of Odysseus.

In the *Iliad*, 'recognition-scenes' are not needed: the heroes generally seem to have no difficulty identifying one another, and if uncertainty exists, an enquiry swiftly yields a frank answer (as with Glaucus and Diomedes). Men in the *Iliad* deal with one another openly and in full awareness of each other's status and strength: even in the dubious *Doloneia*, Odysseus and Diomedes have no need to ask the spy who he is, but know him already (10. 447). It is the gods who deceive, as when Athena tempts Pandarus to break the truce, or Zeus sends a lying dream to Agamemnon. In the *Odyssey*, where the mortals do not deal so honestly with one another, the characters dwell in a state of uncertainty. The suitors speak hypocritically to Penelope and Telemachus, and plan an ambush against the latter; Telemachus deceives his mother and steals away by night; Eumaeus was abducted by his nurse and sold into slavery; Troy was taken by a treacherous device, the Wooden Horse, to which the *Iliad* never refers. So too with the gods: even Athena normally disguises herself when visiting Telemachus or Odysseus, and in book xiii she tests the hero's prowess before revealing herself. The world of the *Odyssey* has a devious and deceptive atmosphere which matches the wily personality of the hero, and with which he is uniquely suited to cope. We come to relish his deceptions and his fluent lying, to delight in the irony as he extracts praise of himself from the wretched Eumaeus, or provokes the hubristic suitors on to further crimes.

After deception, recognition.[41] Telemachus is recognized by Helen in book iv; she also recalls how she once identified Odysseus when he entered Troy in disguise during the siege (iv. 240–56), an episode that seems to anticipate the scene in book xix with Eurycleia and the scar. In Phaeacia Odysseus finally reveals his identity at the opening of book ix. But it is in the second half that the motif becomes more frequent: after the encounter with Athena in xiii, there are recognition-scenes with Telemachus, the dog Argus, Eurycleia, Eumaeus and Philoetius together, the revelation-scene with the suitors, and the climactic scene in which Odysseus and Penelope are re-united, followed by a final pendant in book xxiv, the encounter with his father. These episodes are not randomly distributed. There is a clear contrast between the scenes in which the hero deliberately reveals his identity (e.g. to Telemachus), and those in which he is accidentally exposed (esp. Eurycleia). On the one hand we see and share the hero's superior knowledge, on the other we feel that he is not infallible, but can make mistakes.

There is also a significant relationship between the scene in book xiii, in which Athena tries to make Odysseus give himself away, but unsuccessfully, and the later scene in which Penelope succeeds in upsetting and exposing her husband. Athena, though she deceived Odysseus, was unable to make him lower his guard. Only in book xxiii, in the second encounter with his wife, is the hero finally and incontrovertibly out-tested and out-witted. Here it is Penelope, in her uncertainty and doubt, who conceives a test to see whether Odysseus is truly her husband (xxiii. 108–10, 113–14). Once before, in book xix, she had attempted to do so (xix. 215), but Odysseus had side-stepped. In book xxiii we see the tables turned, the biter bit, when Penelope asks the old nurse to bring out their marital bed for Odysseus to sleep in that night. 'Thus she spoke, testing her husband' (xxiii. 181). At the thought of anyone having tampered with the immovable bed, around which he had built the palace, Odysseus bursts out with open indignation: his famous caution and self-control vanish. The scene thus trumps all Odysseus' previous testing and reverses Penelope's earlier failure. Her success surpasses even the wiles of Athene, the only other female who matches the hero in cleverness and guile.

Finally, the medium of recognition is appropriate in most of the cases: the scar is apt for Eurycleia and the other servants, since they were present when Odysseus came home with that wound; it represents their ties with Odysseus' youth. With Laertes, Odysseus appeals not only to the evidence of the scar, but also to his patrimony, the trees in the orchard where they stand (xxiv. 336 ff.). With Penelope, it is fitting and symbolic that the crucial sign, the proof of Odysseus' return, should be his knowledge of their bed, a shared secret: like their marriage, it is deep-rooted, immovably set, unchanged by time.[42]

Although the *Odyssey* also has a public dimension, in its presentation of Odysseus as the ideal king and of Ithaca as a society disrupted because of his absence,[43] it is arguable that the central family relationships are more important, and that the sensitive presentation of human feelings, both masculine and feminine, goes beyond anything we find in the *Iliad*. This is one reason that many readers have found it an astonishingly modern work, a distant ancestor of the novel.[44]

Men, women, and goddesses[45]

One of the most notorious pronouncements in Homeric studies was the suggestion by Samuel Butler that the *Odyssey* was composed by a woman.[46] Whatever one thinks of the theory itself, it is certainly obvious that female characters are more prominent in the *Odyssey* than in the *Iliad*, where they figure principally as victims of the war, often passive and unspeaking. Chryseis has no opportunity to speak for herself, and Briseis speaks only once, and among her fellow captives, when she mourns the dead Patroclus, unheeded by Achilles (19. 282–302).[47] It is of course true that the goddesses of the poem play a more active part: it would seem that the gulf between mortal and immortal is more important than that between man and woman – though we may ask whether this is equally the case in both epics. But in the *Odyssey* female characters are numerous among both mortals and immortals, and are important in both worlds. In some cases, indeed, the women are cleverer and more effective agents than the men: Helen is shrewder than Menelaus and quicker at recognizing Telemachus, Arete is in some ways more influential in Scheria than Alcinous (vi. 303–15, vii. 53–77). Even on the divine level, Athena's quick-witted appeal to Zeus frustrates her absent uncle Poseidon.[48]

Special interest attaches to Odysseus' dealings and relationships with women. Two of these are divine, Circe and Calypso.[49] It seems that the poet has done his best to differentiate these. Circe, probably the older figure, is a sorceress and a mysterious being, who cannot be fully trusted and with whom the hero forms no real attachment in a year's sojourn. She turns swiftly from threatening witch to generous hostess, but when Odysseus declares that he must leave, she raises no objection. Calypso is a more sympathetic and affectionate figure, devoted to Odysseus and anxious to keep him with her. Her emotions are more human: outrage at the import of Hermes' message, pique at Odysseus' preference for a mortal woman. The scene in which she tries for the last time to prevail on him to stay and accept a life of immortal ease is important in establishing Odysseus' heroic status, but is also a touching and delicate interchange, rich in understated pathos.[50] The gulf between humanity and divinity, tragically exploited in the *Iliad* (especially in the relationship of Achilles and Thetis), here becomes a source of personal sadness, as Calypso accepts abandonment graciously and gives Odysseus the help he must have to depart. It is a pleasing touch that she does not reveal to him the command of Zeus, but leaves him to suppose that she has decided to let him go of her own accord. The theme of dissimulation, ubiquitous in the *Odyssey*, here enables Calypso to preserve her dignity.

There remains Nausicaa, the only human female with whom Odysseus has the opportunity for dalliance (in fact he behaves with perfect propriety).[51] Here again the proximity of the *Odyssey* to 'folk-tale' is evident: a wanderer appears in a strange land, excels in contests, impresses the people of the country and wins the king's daughter.[52] Of course, Odysseus tactfully evades the offer of Nausicaa's hand, though the reader is in no doubt that she is attracted to him (vi. 244–6, vii. 311ff.). Some critics regret that the poet has denied us so charming a romance, but an erotic encounter with Nausicaa would have been a shocking and culpable misdemeanour on Odysseus' part,[53] on quite a different plane from the infidelities with Circe and Calypso: it is rash to deny a deity who offers such favours. The *Odyssey*-poet is prepared to hint that Calypso was not an altogether uncongenial companion in the early years, and we must grant that the epic, like later Greek society, accepts a double standard for the sexual behaviour of men and women, but the importance of fidelity and family ties in this poem have their effect on the hero's character. There is some evidence that Odysseus' *amours* were more numerous in other sources.[54]

The character of Penelope is essential to the plot of the *Odyssey*, and she is clearly the most intriguing female figure in the poem: older descriptions of her as 'a healthy well-nourished lady . . . without any gift of intellect or strength of character' now arouse incredulity and outrage.[55] More recent discussions have laid much more stress on her devotion to her husband, her intelligence, the intensity of her grief, pathetically described in many passages, her attempts to assert her authority, and particularly her satisfying success in outwitting her husband.[56] Recognizing the constraints on her behaviour, as a woman in a male-dominated society, some critics see her as manipulating the men she encounters, using what tools she has and exploiting her very limited range of choices.[57] She can even be seen as enduring in her own sphere sufferings such as heroes undergo: in a simile at iv. 791–3, she is compared to a lion, a comparison normally confined to male characters.[58] Whereas the analysts complained that Penelope's behaviour was inconsistent or inexplicable, readers now admit greater subtleties and see some of the more puzzling scenes as 'provocatively enigmatic'.[59] A more sophisticated model of the poet's allusive technique also helps the interpreter: traditional analysis detected an unhappy conflation of a version in which Penelope did recognize her husband with one in which she did not, but it is perfectly possible that the poet is consistently following one version while playing on his audience's awareness of another. This seems plausible in book xix, where the poet, having brought husband and wife together in a secluded spot at night, seems to be leading us to expect a recognition (as in previous versions of the tale?); but although a recognition does take place in this scene, it is inadvertent, and involves not the queen but the old nurse Eurycleia.

Problematic scenes remain, which cannot be discussed in detail here. Particularly prominent in discussion are the scene in which Penelope extorts gifts from the suitors, the episode in which she converses with the beggar Odysseus but (as is now rightly accepted) fails to recognize her husband (book xix), the passage in which she narrates a dream that foreshadows the doom of the suitors (xix. 535–58), the proposal to hold the contest of the bow, initiated by Penelope with Odysseus' encouragement (572–81), and the final sequence in which she is awakened by the nurse and after initial disbelief eventually accepts that Odysseus has indeed returned (book xxiii). Other puzzling passages include the lines in which one suitor is said to be 'the one who appealed most to Penelope' (xvi. 397 f.), and the speech in which she compares herself, in opaque and elliptical terms, to Helen.[60] All of these shed light on Penelope's personality and emotions: although in some passages we may be surprised or forced to modify our earlier impressions, the fundamental premises of the story, that Penelope is a faithful wife and will re-marry only with deep reluctance, in order to protect Telemachus and his patrimony, should not be questioned.[61] The homecoming of Odysseus would be hollow if that were not so: he has sacrificed even immortality in order to come home to his wife, one who is 'like-minded'. Odysseus himself describes the ideal, in a much earlier passage which sums up several of the poem's fundamental assumptions: 'there is nothing nobler, nothing better, than when man and wife dwell together with their thoughts in common: that brings much grief to their enemies, joy to their friends; and they themselves know it best of all' (vi. 182–5). Their eventual embrace is marked by a simile which is applied to both parties: it starts from Odysseus and finishes with Penelope, and describes their joy in terms of the experiences of a shipwrecked sailor finding his way at last to shore:

These were her words, and she roused still more in him the desire to weep. He cried as he held his beloved wife close to him, that clever woman. As land is welcome when spotted by swimmers whose sturdy vessel Poseidon has wrecked at sea, driven by storm and solid waves – few of them have escaped the grey sea on to land by swimming, and much brine is encrusted on their skin; but gladly they climb on to the shore, escaping from suffering – so glad was the sight of her husband to Penelope, and she still would not release his neck from her white arms' embrace. (xxiii. 231–40)[62]

The linking of Penelope with Odysseus' sufferings stresses not only their reunion, but also the parallels between their different ordeals and achievements – both alone, both enduring, planning, and hoping. Penelope's exceptional qualities are further shown by the calmness with which she accepts that Odysseus must undertake a further journey to placate Poseidon. Past suffering and future parting serve to set their present joy in sharper relief.

The other important female in Odysseus' life is of course the goddess Athena. Theirs was already regarded as a special relationship in the *Iliad* (see esp. 23. 782–3), but in that epic she also befriends other heroes (Achilles and Diomedes). In the *Odyssey* her attention is focussed on a single favourite, and the poet expands this conception to create something almost unique, a close friendship between man and deity. Sometimes she aids him without his knowledge, sometimes more openly; on the whole her interventions become more frequent in the second half. Her interaction with others, even with Telemachus, is more distant, often deceptive: thus in book xv she misleads Telemachus with tales of his mother's eagerness to marry, playing on the young man's fears. In book xviii she puts an impulse in Penelope's mind, and the queen responds without really understanding what she is doing and why. But with Odysseus she is affectionate and reassuring, even teasing, as shown above all in book xiii, where the basis of their relationship is most explicitly defined. She cares for him because they are alike:

> But come, let us talk thus no longer; the two of us both know our tricks – you excel all mankind in stratagem and well-chosen words, while I am renowned among the gods for my wiles and wisdom. Nor did you yourself discern in me Pallas Athene, the daughter of Zeus, I who am always beside you and guard you in all your trials. It was I who endeared you to the Phaeacians; it is I again who am here now to weave a plan together with you . . . (xiii. 296–303)

Although there is doubtless an extra frisson to their relationship because they are male and female, the respect with which Odysseus always speaks to her and the traditional chastity of Athena reduce the significance of this factor: this is a partnership based on intellectual equality. We may contrast both the relationship between Aphrodite and Paris in the *Iliad*, where there is no common ground other than their sensual natures, and the moving portrayal of Hippolytus' devotion to Artemis in the *Hippolytus*, where there is no physical or even visual contact, and indeed no equality: favoured for a time, Hippolytus is left behind to die.[63]

It has sometimes been felt that the constant support and advice of Athena, especially in the second half of the poem, diminish the triumph of the hero.[64] Even with her encouragement, however, he has still to execute his intentions, and it is notable that although she promises her support against the suitors, she gives him no guidance as to how he should win a position of advantage over them. His fluent lying and clever coaxing of help or comforts out of Eumaeus and others need no divine backing. Moreover, in the actual slaughter she abstains from intervention until it is no longer needed: withdrawing from the battle, she observes it from the roof of the hall (xxii. 236–40). In the end she holds up the aegis and sends the suitors running in panic, but by that point the hero and his allies have already gained the upper hand. This is consistent with the practice of the *Iliad* and with later Greek attitudes: the gods help those who are prepared to help themselves.[65]

In one notable respect Athena has the advantage over Penelope: as a goddess, she can take any form she wishes, and in masculine disguise as Mentes or Mentor can play a part in the affairs of Ithaca, organizing a ship for Telemachus and performing other tasks where a woman would be ignored or sent back to her home.[66] As in Aeschylus' *Oresteia*, the goddess who favours the male in all things restores order to a patriarchal society: 'the king's in his palace, all's right with the world'? The masculine personality of the warrior-goddess means that she is even at home in war.

Although such qualities were attributed to the Amazons, who figured in the epic *Aethiopis*, the conventions of Greek family life made it impossible for Penelope to participate in the governing of Ithaca or in state affairs: the most that is possible is for her husband to *compare* her 'renown'[67] with that of a virtuous king whose land is prosperous and governed justly (xix. 108 ff.).[68] It is striking that the word *kleos*, so closely associated with heroic prowess, should be used to describe the passive and domestic virtue of Penelope; but her virtue is still assimilated to, and subordinate to, that of a man, ultimately her husband. Hence for Penelope to have her husband home and her long years of fidelity rewarded means the end of the story. Whether the passage in which husband and wife retire to bed together also marks the end of the epic will be discussed in the next section.

Endings

For the most part it has been assumed above that we are considering a poem which draws upon older sources and traditional material but which is itself shaped by a single mind, a 'monumental poet' who may or may not also be the composer of the *Iliad*. Minor interpolations, sometimes identified by awkwardness or by poor manuscript attestation, do certainly occur, but these are normally a matter of a few lines. Far more significant and disquieting are the doubts which have overshadowed the conclusion of the *Odyssey*, from xxiii. 297 to the end of book xxiv, ever since antiquity.[69] This section embraces the conversation which husband and wife hold in bed together (including an account of his travels); the descent of the suitors to the underworld, where they find Agamemnon and Achilles in conversation, and where the scene ends with Agamemnon congratulating the absent Odysseus on his good fortune, and praising Penelope; the episode in which Odysseus visits his aged father Laertes, tests him in the by-now familiar manner, and eventually reveals himself once Laertes is helpless with grief; and finally, the brief and abortive attempt of the suitors' kinsmen to retaliate against Odysseus and his followers. On the last page of the poem, in a strangely accelerated narrative, Athena and Zeus impose peace on Ithaca. A full review of the problems cannot be given here, but the main issues and their implications should be aired.

The Alexandrian scholars Aristophanes and Aristarchus judged xxiii. 296 to be the 'end' (*telos*) or 'limit' (*peras*) of the *Odyssey*.[70] Arguments that they meant by this not the textual conclusion but the climax or 'goal' of the action are more persuasive with *telos* than with *peras*, and should probably be abandoned.[71] It is much less clear whether they judged the remainder of the poem spurious on textual or internal grounds.[72] Internal difficulties certainly exist, though one does sometimes wonder if modern scholarship would have pursued these with the same ruthlessness if the ancient testimonies had not given them this lead.

The arguments for condemning the section are of different kinds. First there is linguistic usage: the last part of the poem contains many odd forms or unique and difficult expressions which cast doubt on its being authentic work of the main *Odyssey*-poet. Page's exposition of these was severely criticized by Erbse, but Stephanie West, in the most important recent study, has shown that some recalcitrant cases still lack justification and that certain phrases are hard even to understand. Secondly there are arguments from religious belief, especially about the underworld and the afterlife. The debate here is closely related to discussion of book xi, Odysseus' own visit to the land of the dead, which has itself been found controversial.[73] Are the dead conscious or not? Can they converse with one another? Can a dead man enter the underworld before being buried, as the suitors seem to? How coherent is Homer's picture of the afterlife? How consistent should we expect it to be, given that this is imaginative literature and that we find inconsistencies elsewhere in the religious 'system' of the epics? After over-rigid analyses in the past, the recent tendency has been to allow for much more variety and flexibility in Homer's conception of Hades,[74] but Sourvinou-Inwood has now thoroughly re-examined the question, and insists that the picture in book xxiv must derive from a later period than that of book xi and the rest of the *Odyssey*.[75] This conclusion may be contested, but my own feeling is that it significantly shifts the balance of the argument.

Thirdly, and perhaps most important for non-specialists, there is the question of poetic quality. Here of course there is much scope for disagreement. Most people would agree that the scene in the underworld (leaving aside the eschatological difficulties) is a valuable episode: it shows us Odysseus' fellow-heroes once more, and emphasizes their miserable state, whether their deaths were glorious (Achilles) or humiliating (Agamemnon): death is the same for all. Their misfortune is contrasted with Odysseus' triumph, now reunited with wife and son and victorious over his foes. The episode also enables Penelope to be given her due. As for the scene with Laertes, frequent references earlier in the poem have led us to expect an appearance of Odysseus' father,[76] and this is reinforced both by the importance of the father–son theme in the poem and by the potential contrast with the *Iliad*, in which Achilles will never again see his old father and must be content with the momentary union with Priam, an enemy but a mirror-image of Peleus.[77] The way in which Odysseus tests and plays games with his wretched father has outraged many critics, but it should not surprise those who recognize that the hero is not simply a paragon of gentlemanly virtues.[78] By now deception has become second nature to him; nevertheless, as he observes Laertes from a distance he does hesitate, as he never has before, and considers a more open approach. It is consistent with both his character and the thematic tendencies of the poem that he should choose the more devious and potentially more painful option.[79]

The first and last of the four sections are the least satisfactory. Of these the first, in which Odysseus and Penelope recount their stories to one another, is a natural and fitting consequence of their reunion (and story-telling is of course one of the recurring activities of the poem), but the way in which it is narrated is somewhat banal.[80] Far more serious are the charges brought against the conclusion, in which the suitors' relatives summon an assembly, seeking to arouse the community to outrage over the slaughter. Medon and Halitherses warn them not to challenge Odysseus, and they proceed to battle despite this warning. A brief moment of tension is followed by the miraculous charge of Laertes, momentarily restored to youthful strength; in a few more lines the conflict comes to an end, much to Odysseus' satisfaction, and Athena brings harmony to the community. What is peculiar here is that all of the elements seem appropriate and potentially interesting: it is the cursory and over-hasty execution that fails to satisfy, particularly after so leisurely an episode at Laertes' farm. It is almost as though this last section, and in particular the last 60 lines, were a rough sketch which was awaiting further elaboration. Neither the supporters nor the opponents of the Continuation have adequately explained this strange unevenness of style.

Two passages earlier in the *Odyssey* seem to prepare for the events of book xxiv, making reference to the danger from the suitors' kinsmen and the prospect of Odysseus visiting his father (xx. 41–3, xxiii. 137–9). Those who see the Continuation as a later composition must argue that these lines too are interpolated, or that they refer to an earlier version which also contained these events. Defenders of the Continuation often claim that it picks up ideas or develops themes present in the earlier part of the epic, but analysts can dispose of this argument with ease, by maintaining that this is obviously what an imitator would do. Thus the scene in the Ithacan assembly clearly builds on book ii (where Halitherses also appeared), but that does not guarantee the authenticity of book xxiv. Similarly the second underworld scene develops themes of book xi (especially the superiority of

Odysseus' career to that of Achilles), but that need not mean they are by the same hand.[81]

Perhaps the most substantial question arising from this debate is whether the *Odyssey* originally ended with Odysseus and Penelope in bed together, in which case the poet is treating the continuity of their marriage as all-important, or with the aftermath of the slaughter, with potential civil war in Ithaca averted – clearly, a more public and political finale. The answer will be different depending on which passages the critic selects and emphasizes from the earlier stages of the poem. But it is hard to believe that nothing was said about the reclaiming of the kingdom, though some have maintained that epic values would not necessarily require an avenging hero to give any justification for his actions, and that it was only in the later stages of the tradition, when kingship was giving way to aristocratic government, that the need was felt to provide some statement of how the community of Ithaca reacted to the extermination of 110 suitors. In the past I have generally felt that the good parts of the Continuation outweighed the bad, but some of the recent discussions have made me feel that it is more likely to be the work of a later poet. Nevertheless, I continue to think that the tale is unlikely to have ended as Aristarchus and Aristophanes maintained, and that since it is necessary to take their statement seriously, we should allow that something has gone wrong in the tradition, and that an older conclusion has been either lost or reworked, perhaps abbreviated in its final stages. The exact process involved is of course beyond us, but there has clearly been some thought given to the integration of the ending, in view of the anticipatory passages already cited. Hence the tenth book of the *Iliad* is not truly parallel,[82] for the most striking fact about that book is that it can be removed with no adjustment to the surrounding text.

If the Continuation is rejected, then the 'authentic' *Odyssey* reaches its climax with the violent revenge of the hero, at his most Iliadic, upon his enemies and on those who have betrayed him;[83] it then proceeds to a conclusion in a gentler and more subtle style, with dialogue more significant than action, in the recognition and reunion of husband and wife. It thus shows Odysseus supreme in battle but also successful in peace. Although Penelope would be denied the words of commendation which she receives from Agamemnon in book xxiv, the sequence of recognitions would end with hers, in which she emerges as the 'victor', and the poem would end with celebration of their marital union. Debate over the merits and status of the existing conclusion will no doubt continue, but xxiii. 296 is an ending we may be able to learn to live with.

NOTES

1. The standard commentary for scholars is now Heubeck et al. (originally published with a text, and in a more attractive format, in Italian (6 vols., 1981–6); now translated and publ. in 3 vols. by Oxford 1988–92). The first volume is the most valuable, with important introductory essays. See also Jones 1991, for books 1 and 2; more advanced, Garvie 1994 on books 6–8, Rutherford 1992 on books 19 and 20. Jones 1988 is an unpretentious and informative guide to the poem aimed at readers of Lattimore's translations. For book-length studies see H. W. Clarke, *The Art of the Odyssey* (New Jersey, 1967; repr. with additions Bristol, 1989), Thornton 1970, Eisenberger 1973, Austin 1975, Griffin 1987, S. V. Tracy, *The Story of the Odyssey* (Princeton, 1990; rather elementary), U. Hölscher, *Die Odyssee: Epos zwischen Märchen und Roman* (Munich, 1989). G. E. Dimock, Jr., *The Unity of the Odyssey* (Amherst, 1989) is a book-by-book reading, sometimes rather disappointing: see my review in *CR* 41 (1991), 9–10. Page 1973 is an enjoyable essay on the adventures of books 9–12 (cf. 1955, ch. 1). Hölscher 1939 and esp. Fenik 1974 are indispensable on the thematic structure. A good deal of the material in part 1 of Edwards 1987 concerns both epics.

2. For a fuller treatment of the topics covered in this section see Rutherford 1991–3; also A. Heubeck, *Der Odyssee-Dichter und die Ilias* (Erlangen, 1954); W. Burkert, 'Das Lied von Ares und Aphrodite', *RhM* 103 (1960), 130–44; Griffin 1987, 63–70, and (most fully) K. Usener, *Beobachtungen zum Verhältnis der Odyssee zur Ilias* (ScriptOralia 21, Tübingen, 1990) (reviewed by Griffin, *CR* 41, 1991, 288–91).

3. Sen. *de brev. vitae* 13. 2 refers to the argument over priority as one of the pointless debates of Greek scholarship. Page 1955, 149–59 argued for complete independence, but has not generally been followed.

4. For the problems of the conclusion of the *Odyssey* see pp. 74–7 below.

5. On Odysseus in the *Iliad* see further Stanford 1963, chh. 2–5; E. K. Borthwick, *Odyssean Elements in the Iliad* (Edinburgh, 1985).

6. F. Cairns, *Virgil's Augustan Epic* (Cambridge, 1990), ch. 8, attempts to argue that the *Odyssey* had a higher status in some periods of antiquity than the *Iliad*.

7. Cf. Goldhill 1991, 1–68; Rutherford 1991–3, 48–9; Segal 1995, chh. 6–8.

8. See now S. D. Olson, *Blood and iron: story and story-telling in Homer's Odyssey* (Leiden, Mnemos. Supplement 148, 1995).

9. On Odysseus' lies see C. Emlyn-Jones, 'True and lying tales in the *Odyssey*', *G&R* 33 (1986), 1–10, Goldhill 1991, 36–48, Rutherford 1992, 69–73.

10. Juvenal 15. 13–26, Lucian *True History* 1. 3, Dio Chr. 11. 34; cf. Goldhill 1991, 47–8.

11. Indeed, the narrative itself contradicts this interpretation as far as the Cyclops-tale is concerned: see esp. i. 20–1 with 68–75, v. 282 ff.

12. Cf. W. Marg, 'Das erste Lied des Demodokos', in *Navicula Chilonensis* (Fest. F. Jacoby) (Leiden, 1956), 16–29, Macleod 1982, 1–8, 1983, ch. 1; differently G. Nagy, *The Best of the Achaeans* (Baltimore, 1979), 42–58.

13. See further Burkert (n. 2 above), B. K. Braswell, 'The song of Ares and Aphrodite: theme and relevance to Odyssey 8' *Hermes* 90 (1982), 129–37, and the notes in Garvie's commentary.

14. W. Mattes, *Odysseus bei den Phäaken. Kritisches zur Homeranalyse* (Würzburg, 1958), esp. 129 ff.; reservations in Fenik 1974, 13–18. See now Garvie 1994, 26–30.

15. Cf. G. Steiner, 'Homer and the scholars', in *Language and Silence* (London, 1967), 221: 'it reminds one of the performance of an air from "The Marriage of Figaro" in the last act of "Don Giovanni"'.

16. On the importance of naming and anonymity in the *Odyssey* see N. Austin, 'Name magic in the *Odyssey*', *CSCA* 5 (1972), 1–19; Fenik 1974, 5–60; Goldhill 1991, 24–36; I. J. F. de Jong, 'Studies in Homeric denomination', *Mnemos.* 46 (1993), 289–306.

17. Rüter 1969, 228–46; Rutherford 1985; Garvie 1994, introd.

18. See further Hölscher 1939, 37–50.

19. M. J. Apthorp, 'The obstacles to Odysseus' return', *CQ* 30 (1980) 1–22; Hoesktra on xv. 1 ff.

20. Scenes such as 15. 142–261 provide a partial precedent, but on a much shorter time-scale. See Krischer 1971, 131 ff.; C. H. Whitman and R. Scodel, 'Sequence and simultaneity in *Iliad* N, Ξ and O', *HSCP* 85 (1981), 1–15; Janko on 14. 1–152.

21. Odysseus' self-description on two occasions in the *Iliad* as 'the father of Telemachus' is

abnormal procedure in that epic, and seems to imply that this relationship was already important in earlier poetry. It is probably relevant that Telemachus is the only son of an only son (xvi. 118–20).
22. Schol. i. 93 and 284. For doubts see S. West 1988, 54–5.
23. Note also the fate of the lesser Ajax, described at iv. 499–511. See further F. Klingner, 'Über die vier ersten Bücher der Odyssee', *SAW* Leipzig, Phil.-hist. Kl. 96, 1 (Leipzig, 1944) = *Studien zur griechischen und römischen Literatur* (Zürich-Stuttgart, 1964), 39–79.
24. E. F. D'Arms and K. K. Hulley, 'The Oresteia-story in the *Odyssey*', *TAPA* 77 (1946), 207–13; U. Hölscher, 'Die Atridensage in der Odyssee', *Festschrift für R. Alewyn*, edd. H. Singer and B. von Wiese (Cologne, 1967), 1–16; S. West 1988, 56–7, 60.
25. M. Müller, *Athene als göttliche Helferin in der Odyssee* (Heidelberg, 1966).
26. For the novelty of the sentiments expressed see Finley 1954 (2nd edn. 1978), 140–1. More generally on the morality of the *Odyssey* see J. M. Redfield in Rubino-Shelmerdine 1983, esp. 239–44; Rutherford 1986, 156.
27. Dodds 1951, 28–37. Contrast Fenik 1974, 208–30. For other views see bibl. in S. West on i. 32 ff.; Erbse 1986, 237–41; Kullmann 1985; R. Friedrich, 'Thrinakia and Zeus' ways of God to men in the Odyssey', *GRBS* 28 (1987), 375–400; M. Winterbottom, 'Speaking of the Gods', *G&R* 26 (1989), 33 41; R. Hankey, '"Evil" in the Odyssey', in E. W. Craik (ed.), *Owls to Athens: Essays . . . Sir Kenneth Dover* (Oxford, 1990), 87–96; C. Segal, 'Divine Justice in the *Odyssey*: Cyclops, Helios and Poseidon', *AJP* 113 (1992), 489–518 = Segal 1995, 195–227 (strongly unitarian).
28. J. S. Clay, *The Wrath of Athena* (Princeton, 1983) perversely argues that Odysseus' misfortunes are the result of Athena's anger with her protégé. This has not been generally accepted, but her book contains many good observations on Homer's gods.
29. On most of these episodes see Radermacher 1915, Page 1973; also the works cited in n. 37 below.
30. As already remarked by Eratosthenes ap. Strabo i. 2.15–17. See further Walbank on Polyb. 34. 2–4, Luce in Stanford-Luce 1974, 118–38; H. H. and A. Wold, *Der Weg des Odysseus* (Tübingen, 1968).
31. Reinhardt 1948.
32. For the importance of Agamemnon see p. 63 above; for the silent departure of Ajax see p. 94 below.
33. See e.g. Rüter 1969, 251 ff.; Wender 1978, 41–4; Griffin 1980, 100–1; J. S. Clay, *The Wrath of Athena: Gods and Man in the Odyssey* (Princeton, 1983), 108 ff.; Goldhill 1991, 104–6. Some aspects of the differences of outlook between the *Odyssey* and the *Iliad* are discussed further in Rutherford 1991–3.
34. On the question of Odysseus' death (violent or peaceful?) see A. Hartmann, *Untersuchungen über die Sagen vom Tod des Odysseus* (Munich, 1917); Stanford 1963, 86–9; Heubeck on xi. 134b–7.
35. For what follows see esp. Vidal-Naquet 1970, rev. 1981.
36. Cf. C. Segal, 'Transition and ritual in Odysseus' return', *PP* 22 (1967), 321–42, and id., 'The Phaeacians and the symbolism of Odysseus' return', *Arion* 1 (1962), 17–64 (both revised in Segal 1995, chh. 2–4); Fenik 1974, 54–5; Garvie 1994, 22–5. For the hedonism see esp. viii. 246–9; M. Dickie, 'Phaeacian athletes', *PLLS* 4 (Liverpool, 1983), 237–76.
37. Calhoun 1939; Page 1955, 18 n. 1; Stith Thompson, *Motif Index of Folk Literature* (Copenhagen, 1955–8), N681, H331; W. Crooke, 'Some notes on Homeric folk-lore', *Folklore* 19 (1908), 52–77, 153–89, and 'The Wooing of Penelope', *Folklore* 9 (1898), 97 ff., V. Zhirmunsky, 'The Epic of "Alpamysh" and the Return of Odysseus', *PBA* 52 (1966), 267–86. For different analogies see W. Burkert, 'Von Amenophis II zur Bogenprobe des Odyssee', *Grazer Beiträge* 1 (1973), 69–78.
38. See Rutherford on xix. 380–1 on the question whether Odysseus is recognizable or not.
39. See further Radermacher 1915; Page 1973, 55, 69 etc.
40. See Fenik 1974, 5–60, Stewart 1976, Murnaghan 1987.
41. N. J. Richardson, 'Recognition-scenes in the *Odyssey* and ancient criticism', *PLLS* 4 (1983), 219–35.
42. See further Whitman 1958, 300–5, Wender 1978, 60–2. For a semiotic reading of Odysseus' bed see Zeitlin in Cohen 1995, 117–52.
43. Thornton 1970, ch. 6; Austin 1975, 162–71. This aspect seems to me understated by S. West 1988, 59–60; contrast Rutherford 1992, 13–15.
44. Cf. Stanford 1963: note especially the well-known claim by Joyce that Odysseus was a truly rounded character, more so even than Hamlet or Faust (quoted in R. Ellmann, *James Joyce* (Oxford, 1966; 2nd edn. 1982), 435–6); see also Ellmann, *Ulysses on the Liffey* (Oxford and N.Y., 1974, revised 1984), H. Kenner, *Ulysses* (London, 1980, rev. 1987).

45. The fertile field of classical scholarship on women cannot be sifted here: see e.g. G. Clark's helpful *G&R* Survey (Oxford 1980, 2nd ed. 1993), and the forthcoming *G&R Studies* volume on this topic, ed. I. McAuslan and P. Walcot (Oxford, 1996); M. R. Lefkowitz, *Heroines and hysterics* (London, 1991) and *Women in Greek Myth* (London, 1995); J. Peradotto and J. P. Sullivan (edd.), *Women in the Ancient World: the Arethusa Papers* (Albany, 1984); A. Cameron and A. Kuhrt (edd.), *Images of Women in Antiquity* (London, 1983, rev. 1993).

46. Butler, *The Authoress of the Odyssey* (1897, 2nd edn. 1922); see also R. Graves, *Homer's Daughter* (N.Y. and London, 1955). Butler's outlook is discussed satirically from a modern standpoint by Winkler 1990, 129 ff.

47. The admiration of Taplin (which in most respects I endorse) for the *Iliad* goes much too far when he claims that the sympathetic treatment of women in that poem makes it *more* likely than the *Odyssey* to be a woman's work (1992, 32).

48. See further M. Detienne and J.-P. Vernant, *Les ruses d'intelligence: la métis des grecs* (Paris, 1974; Eng. tr. *Cunning Intelligence in Greek Culture and Society*, Brighton, 1978).

49. See esp. G. Crane, *Calypso: backgrounds and conventions of the Odyssey* (Frankfurt am Main, 1988), with ample refs. to older discussions.

50. See also Griffin 1980, 59–61, esp. 59 n. 17.

51. See now Garvie 1994, 29–30.

52. Woodhouse 1930, ch. 7, R. Lattimore, 'Nausikaa's Suitors', in *Classical Studies presented to B. E. Perry* (Urbana, Chicago, London, 1969), 88–102, H. Petersmann, 'Homer und das Märchen', *WS* 15 (1981), 43–68.

53. See esp. Stanford 1963, 51 ff., against the sentimentality of Woodhouse 1930, 64.

54. E.g. with the queen of the Thesprotians in the Cyclic *Telegony*.

55. Woodhouse 1930, 201.

56. The secondary literature is already enormous, and much remains unpublished. In general on the mythical figure of Penelope see M. Mactoux, *Pénélope: légende et mythe* (Paris, 1975); on her presentation in Homer, W. Büchner, 'Die Penelopeszenen in der Odyssee', *Hermes* 75 (1940), 126–67; P. W. Harsh, 'Penelope and Odysseus in *Odyssey* xix', *AJP* 71 (1950), 1–21 (an enjoyable but misguided attempt to prove that Penelope did indeed recognize her husband on his return); A. Amory, 'The reunion of Odysseus and Penelope', in Taylor 1963, 100–21 (important for moving the debate on to a more subtle psychological level); H. Vester, 'Das 19. Buch der Odyssee', *Gymn.* 75 (1968), 417–34; Austin 1975, ch. 4; Emlyn-Jones 1984; J. Russo, introd. to the English edn. of his comm. on *Odyssey* xvii–xx, 3–16; Winkler 1990, 129–61; M. A. Katz, *Penelope's Renown. Meaning and indeterminacy in the Odyssey* (Princeton, 1991; deconstructive reading), N. Felson-Rubin, 'Penelope's perspective: character from plot' in Bremer et al. 1987, 61–83, and *Regarding Penelope: from character to poetics* (Princeton, 1993) (combining psychology and narratology), and Murnaghan and Zeitlin in Cohen 1995. I have not greatly changed my views as stated in Rutherford 1992, 27–38, though I grant that some of the more recent work is provocative and stimulating.

57. Winkler 1990, 142–3.

58. See further H. Foley, ' "Reverse similes" and sex roles in the *Odyssey*', *Arethusa* 11 (1978), 7–26 = Peradotto and Sullivan (see n. 45 above), 59–78.

59. Felson-Rubin in Bremer et al. 1987, 82.

60. xxiii. 218–24, defended by Heubeck ad loc., but by few others.

61. The cynical view that Penelope was not faithful to Odysseus was already current in antiquity: see e.g. Hor. *Satires* 2.5.78–83, Sen. *Epist.* 88. 8 (the latter passage also refers to the debate about whether she recognized her husband or not).

62. For other parallels between husband and wife see Rutherford 1986, 160 n. 77.

63. See esp. Eur. *Hipp.* 85–6, 1389–1401, 1437–41 (J.-P. Vernant, *Mythe et pensée chez les grecs*, Paris, 1965, tr. as *Myth and Thought among the Greeks*, London, 1983, ch. 14). Even the Odysseus–Athena relationship is given something of this chilly remoteness in the prologue to Sophocles' *Ajax*.

64. See e.g. Kirk 1962, 365, 378–9.

65. Cf. Fraenkel's note on Aesch. *Agam.* 811; J. D. Mikalson, *Athenian Popular Religion* (Chapel Hill, 1983), ch. 2.

66. For comparison between Athena and Penelope see also Murnaghan in Cohen 1995, 68–73.

67. xix. 108 *kleos*, and cf. 128 = xviii. 255. See further Foley (n. 58), 11 ff.; C. Segal, '*Kleos* and its ironies in the *Odyssey*', *AC* 52 (1983), 22–47 (repr. in Segal 1995, 84–109); A. T. Edwards 1985, 78–82; Goldhill 1991, 93 ff., arguing for 'revisionist' use of the vocabulary of fame; I.

Papadopoulou-Belmehdi, *Le chant de Pénélope: Poétique de tissage féminin dans l'Odyssée* (Paris, 1994).

68. That Arete does have some say in these matters is another oddity about the Phaeacian community; and it is notable that in fact she does little to justify her reputation, and that when she does initiate a proposal she is told firmly by Echeneus that 'On Alcinous here depends deed and word' (xi. 346, cf. Finley 1954, rev. 1978, 89; Garvie on vi. 310–15).

69. See Heubeck on xxiii. 296 for basic arguments and bibliography; the modern assailants are best represented by Page 1955, ch. 5 (overstating his case, and with many purely rhetorical arguments); S. West 1989; R. Oswald, *Das Ende der Odyssee. Studien zu Strukturen epischen Gestaltens* (diss. Graz, 1993). Defenders include esp. Heubeck in his commentary, Erbse 1972, 97–109, 166–244, C. Moulton, 'The end of the *Odyssey*', *GRBS* 15 (1974), 139–52, H.-A. Stössel, *Der letzte Gesang der Odyssee* (diss. Erlängen-Nuremberg, 1975), Wender 1978.

70. Their views are quoted by the scholia and Eustathius; see e.g. S. West 1989, 118 for the relevant passages.

71. So Pfeiffer 1968, 175; see now S. West 1989, 118–9.

72. S. West ibid. argues they did not even think it spurious, but saw it as a separate lay by the poet. This does not, however, much affect the modern debate.

73. See further G. Petzl, *Antiken Diskussionen über die beiden Nekyiai* (Meisenheim, 1969); C. Sourvinou-Inwood, 'Crime and punishment: Tityos, Tantalos and Sisyphos in *Odyssey* 11', *BICS* 33 (1986), 37–58.

74 Older views e.g. in E. Rohde, *Psyche* (Eng. tr. London and N.Y., 1925), ch. 1; Page 1955, 21–7. More flexibility: e.g. Vermeule 1979, 29, 34–5, 218 n. 49 (cf. S. West 1989, 138 n. 51); also an Oxford D. Phil. thesis (1995) by M. Clark, which will, I hope, soon be published.

75. Sourvinou-Inwood 1995, ch. 2, esp. 94–107.

76. S. West 1989 argues that these are all interpolated by the author of this section, but this is not the most persuasive part of her paper.

77. Cf. Rutherford 1986, 162 n. 87.

78. Cf. P. Walcot, 'Odysseus and the art of lying', *Anc. Soc.* 8 (1977), 1–19 = Emlyn-Jones et al. 1992, 49–62.

79. Hence I do not agree with S. West 1989, 125, who writes that 'We should of course all like to avoid this conclusion' [i.e. that Odysseus is now habitually a deceiver].

80. Wender 1978, 15–18 attempts to defend it, but succeeds only in some small details. S. West 1989, 121 points out that Odysseus' narrative here, 310–43, is the longest piece of indirect speech in all of Homer (though see K. J. Dover, *Lysias and the Corpus Lysiacum* (Berkeley and Los Angeles, 1968), 96, for the limited value of such arguments).

81. Thus Sourvinou-Inwood 1995, 101.

82. Cf. S. West 1989, 120, and on the *Doloneia* see p. 19 above.

83. Modern readers are repelled by the mutilation of the disloyal Melanthius (on which see now M. Davies, '*Odyssey* 22. 474–7: murder or mutilation', *CQ* 44 (1994), 534–6) and by the hanging of the maids. By contrast with the seriousness with which the *Iliad* surrounds the issue of mutilation (Segal, 1971), the *Odyssey* seems remarkably casual (cf. Murray 1907, 4th edn. 1934, 126–8, who surely misinterprets the tone of xxii. 473). Perhaps one simply has to accept that Homer's audience would have thought any punishment justifiable for such treachery within the household.

IV. SOME MEMORABLE SCENES

In the remaining pages I shall offer some more detailed comments on a number of passages from both epics. Besides allowing slightly more attention to stylistic matters than was possible in the earlier chapters, this procedure also gives an opportunity to comment on some specific problems, and on a number of other approaches which have not been discussed so far.

Iliad 3. 424–47

And Aphrodite, smiling goddess, herself took up a chair for Helen, and brought it and placed it in front of Alexandros [Paris]. There Helen, daughter of Zeus who wields the aegis, took her seat, turning her eyes aside, and spoke slightingly to her husband: 'You came back from the fighting, then. I wish you had died there, brought down by a man of strength, who was once my husband. Oh, before now you used to boast that you were superior to the warrior Menelaus in strength and power of hand and spear. Well, go now, challenge the warrior Menelaus to fight you again face to face. But no, I would advise you to stop now, and not pit yourself against fair-haired Menelaus in warfare or combat without thinking – you might well be brought down by his spear.'

Paris then answered her: 'Wife, do not deride my courage with these hard taunts. This time Menelaus has beaten me with Athena's aid, but another time I shall beat him: there are gods on our side too. No, come, let us enjoy the bed of love. Never before has desire so enveloped my heart, not even on that first time when I stole you away from lovely Lacedaimon and sailed off with you in my seafaring ships, and lay with you in love's union in the island of Kranae – even that was less than the love and sweet desire for you that comes over me now.'

So he spoke, and led the way to their bed: and his wife followed. (Tr. M. Hammond)

Later readers thought it implausible that a ten-year war should be undertaken to recover a faithless wife, and in Greek lyric and tragedy Helen generally receives unfriendly treatment.[1] The Trojan elders gaze admiringly at her as she appears on the walls, but their attitude is divided: it is no cause for reproach that Greeks and Trojans should fight over such a woman, and yet it would be better if she left and returned home (3. 156–60). Helen herself comments that the women of Troy, not surprisingly, regard her with deep hostility (3. 411–2, 24. 768–70, 774–5). But Helen's own attitude has been found ambiguous by many. Uncertainty surrounds the original flight with Paris: was she abducted against her will, or did she come with him voluntarily? The repeated line in which Greeks are said to be 'avenging the struggles and moaning of Helen' (2. 356 = 590), though it can be twisted to mean their own struggles over her, is more naturally read as implying that she left Sparta reluctantly; but it is possible that this is a misguided opinion, even a kind of wishful thinking on the part of the speakers. That Paris was also able to carry off much treasure (e.g. 7. 363–4) suggests that the 'abduction' was not a violent or rapid process, but involved cooperation on Helen's part. Most important of all are Helen's own comments on her actions. In each of the three episodes in which she appears, she blames herself and wishes that she had died before she came to Troy; although she speaks with respect and affection to Priam and Hector (and values their gentle treatment of her), she is bitter and contemptuous towards Paris. All of this suggests that she feels considerable responsibility and guilt over her original departure – that, in short, she was sufficiently infatuated with Paris to make what has proved to be a disastrous choice, abandoning her husband and child for a lesser man.[2]

The extract above follows on Aphrodite's rescue of Paris from seemingly certain death at Menelaus' hands. His efforts on the field were inglorious, his 'withdrawal' seems to ensure a Greek victory, given the terms laid down for the duel. Helen comes to him reluctantly: Aphrodite has first cajoled and then, meeting a defiant reply, has threatened her, effectively forcing her to come to Paris's bedchamber. Aphrodite is in control of the situation, acting to bring pleasure to Paris, her favourite. Helen's distaste is indicated by her turning her eyes away, and by the sharpness of her opening line; her repeated references to her former husband make clear that she is still, as earlier in the episode, full of longing for the past that she has left behind in Greece (cf. 3. 139–40, 173–80, 232–3, 236–44).

In view of this, it is surprising that some readers have detected a change of tone at 433 ('But no, I would advise you ...'), assuming that this represents a softening on Helen's part: yes, Menelaus is the better man, and yet her love is still for Paris.[3] Is her conclusion a sign of resurgent affection and concern, or a sarcastic and sceptical comment ('no, I don't think you would be wise to do that')? We should note the disparaging adverb 'foolishly' in 436 (Hammond's 'without thinking' is probably too mild); this, and the fact that Paris himself refers to her speech as 'hard taunts' (438), seem to support the latter interpretation. It is Paris who is passionate in this scene; Helen in his chamber remains as reluctant as when she spoke out against Aphrodite. Paris is the comical, lustful figure, in contrast with Helen, a tragic victim.

The other reading, which sees Helen as overwhelmed by passion and returning willingly to Paris's arms, is undoubtedly influenced by the presence of Aphrodite throughout the episode. The goddess of love, it is argued, must have the power to alter a mortal woman's feelings; is this not what Aphrodite does here with Helen? Important for this argument is the line which follows Aphrodite's approach to Helen on the walls: 'thus she spoke, and stirred *thumon* (emotion? enthusiasm?) in her [Helen's] breast' (3. 395). What emotion is kindled here – desire or anger? Parallel passages give limited help here: elsewhere, it is true, this expression seems to indicate that the listener is convinced or stimulated to do what the speaker has advised,[4] but it is not certain that this must be the case wherever the line is used: moreover, this is a less straightforward situation, as in the other cases the speaker is a mortal addressing a mortal, and there is normally no reason to doubt that the other will respond (11. 804 is perhaps the closest analogy to the present passage). Perhaps it is a mistake to try to identify the emotion precisely: does the line mean more than 'Thus Aphrodite spoke, and Helen was moved by what she said'?

A subtle and ingenious interpretation, which owes something to the school of 'neo-analysis' discussed below (p. 91), sees this scene as a re-enactment of Helen's original crime.[5] As Aphrodite prompted her to leave with Paris in the first place (or, in human terms, in the same way that she fell in love with her glamorous foreign guest), so now, though years afterwards, despite Helen's longing for Menelaus, Aphrodite brings her back to Paris's bed. This theory gains some support from the fact that Aphrodite at first takes the form of an old woman, a wool-worker, who served Helen in Sparta: perhaps she played the part of a go-between at the time of the original seduction? The parallelism would be a further example of the way in which episodes of the early years of the war are recalled or remoulded in the early books of the *Iliad* (p. 30 above). But in the absence of a narration by the *Iliad*-poet of the seduction, the theory must remain speculation. Even if the parallel is allowed, the differences between the scenes are at least as important. If line 395 does imply some renewal of Helen's desire for Paris, it is swiftly dispelled; Aphrodite's influence upon her emotions is ineffectual, and the goddess must resort to threats. If Helen does soften and go willingly to bed with Paris, the poet gives us no clear indication of this: the final line of the scene is carefully neutral (447). When we next see Helen with Paris, he is cheerfully playing with his armour rather than putting it on, and she is again bitter in reproach of herself and her lover (6. 321–2, 343–58). While it may be wrong to deny any hint whatsoever of erotic attraction on Helen's side, any such passion on her part is short-lived and joyless.

This scene, then, is a particularly complex test-case for discussion of the interplay between human psychology and divine intervention, a topic treated in ch. 2. I have argued that Helen's emotions are her own, and that she no longer feels any emotional involvement with Paris. Other positions are possible, and this may be a case where the poet has deliberately allowed some ambiguity. It remains important that Helen tries to reject Aphrodite's overtures, and is critical of Paris. If this were not so, she would be a much less sympathetic character.

Lighter aspects of the scene may be found in the reaction of Paris to Helen's rebuke. His declaration that Menelaus has won 'with Athena's aid', while he will have his chance another day, is particularly shameless from one who only escaped death through Aphrodite's aid; nor did the poet give us any hint of Athena's involvement in Menelaus' onslaught. The reference to Paris's passionate desire for Helen, which led him to make love to her at the first opportunity 'on a rocky island',[6] humorously enhances our sense of his frivolous sensuality. The scene is a close relation of the amorous encounter between the lustful Zeus and the less enthusiastic Hera in book 14 (cf. esp. 3. 442–6 with 14. 315–28); but there the goddess is deliberately setting out to deceive her husband, whereas here the woman has no power to resist.[7] Moreover, the whole scene is a witty inversion of a 'typical' situation in Homeric epic. It is common for a woman to restrain a man, trying to prevent him from going out to battle or into danger.[8] Thus Andromache does her best to induce Hector to remain in Troy, and Hecuba begs Priam not to go to confront Achilles; in the *Odyssey*, Eurycleia tries to persuade Telemachus not to set out in search of his father. In all these cases the man resists these overtures and shows himself a hero. But in book 3 the motif is reversed, for Helen, disgusted at Paris's poor showing in battle, tells him to go out and fight like a man, whereupon he replies that he will not go, and urges her to come to bed (cf. also 6. 337–8). Comic and enjoyable in itself, the scene gains in sophistication if we see it as a clever adaptation of familiar material.

Iliad 9. 478–97

> And away I fled through the whole expanse of Hellas
> and gaining the good dark soil of Phthia, mother of flocks,
> I reached the king, and Peleus gave me a royal welcome.
> Peleus loved me as a father loves a son, I tell you,
> his only child, the heir to his boundless wealth,
> he made me a rich man, he gave me throngs of subjects,
> I ruled the Dolopes, settling down on Phthia's west frontier.
> And I made you what you are – strong as the gods, Achilles –
> I loved you from the heart. You'd never go with another
> to banquet on the town or feast in your own halls.
> Never, until I'd sat you down on my knees
> and cut you the first bits of meat, remember?

You'd eat your fill, I'd hold the cup to your lips
and all too often you soaked the shirt on my chest,
spitting up some wine, a baby's way . . . a misery.
Oh I had my share of troubles for you, Achilles,
did my share of labour. Brooding, never forgetting
the gods would bring no son of mine to birth,
not from my own loins. So you, Achilles –
great, godlike Achilles – I made you my son, I tried,
so someday *you* might fight disaster off my back.
But now, Achilles, beat down your mounting fury!
It's wrong to have such an iron, ruthless heart . . . (tr. R. Fagles)

The long speech of Phoenix, Achilles' mentor, has already been mentioned in ch. 1 (p. 7 above). He is the second of the embassy to make an appeal to Achilles, coming between Odysseus and Ajax. His is the longest speech: like Nestor, he tends to garrulousness. Whereas Odysseus had used arguments based on profit and prestige, Phoenix addresses his former protégé in emotional and personal terms, narrating his own life history, recalling the bonds between him and Achilles, producing moral arguments backed up by quaint allegory, and telling the story of Meleager as a warning to Achilles: his example shows the dangers of intransigent anger.[9] The rather sentimental tone evident in this extract annoys Achilles (612 'do not try to disturb me by weeping and complaining'), and he resents the fact that Phoenix of all people should be siding with his enemy (613–14); but he does make a concession in replying to Phoenix. Whereas in his answer to Odysseus he had declared that he would set off home next day, he now says that in the morning 'we shall consider whether to go back to our own lands or to remain' (618–19). In reaction to Ajax's short and contemptuous speech he goes still further. Phoenix, therefore, has an important part to play in book 9. Particularly important is the prominence of the father-son theme in his speech: he treats Achilles as the son he never had (note esp. 437 'dear child'), and Achilles responds with the pet-name *atta* ('dada', 607). The failure of Phoenix, an old man who has been like a father to Achilles, is countered in book 24 by the success of Priam, a still more pitiful old man who wins over Achilles by comparing himself with Peleus, the hero's father (24. 486–506).[10]

There is, however, a problem surrounding the membership of the embassy, and this is a case where the difficulties felt by the analysts cannot be waved away by either unitarian or oralist critics. It is not simply that Phoenix is a character unmentioned before book 9: new characters are often introduced according to the poet's needs. Nestor refers to the embassy as consisting of Phoenix, who is to be the leader, Ajax, and

Odysseus (they are to be accompanied by two heralds). But when they are proceeding along the shore, and when they arrive in Achilles' encampment, the ambassadors are repeatedly referred to in the dual form ('the two of them') – nine times in less than twenty lines (182–99).[11] Soon afterwards the poet mentions Odysseus (218); and in line 223 all three names appear ('Ajax nodded to Phoenix, but godlike Odysseus noticed . . .'). From that point on the episode unfolds without difficulty; but we remain baffled by the shift between an embassy of three and one of two (most interpreters agree that the heralds can be ignored).[12] The conclusion seems inescapable that a version once existed which involved only two ambassadors, and the majority of critics think of Phoenix as the interloper. The analysts simply assumed that a later hand had added Phoenix; the elaborate theory of Page, in fact, identifies at least four layers, an *Iliad* without any embassy, then an embassy of two, then the version with Phoenix, then the addition of book 19 (there are further subtleties). But Phoenix is more important and less easily dispensable than Page maintained: even without looking outside book 9, if we omit the speech of Phoenix and Achilles' reply, the latter's concession to Ajax becomes inexplicably sudden. A different approach, starting from the assumption that a master-poet lies behind the work as a whole, imagines the *Iliad* as gradually developing in Homer's hands: the embassy book evolved, and Phoenix, while a later addition, was still added by the monumental poet, and integrated in the poem.[13] On this argument, the duals offer us a glimpse into 'Homer's workshop'.[14] That argument gains some support from the fact that Achilles' instructor is elsewhere said to have been Chiron the centaur, a supernatural figure (11. 832, cf. 16. 143 = 19. 390), whereas here he is given a human teacher. As we have seen elsewhere, it seems to be characteristic of Homer, and especially the *Iliad*, to play down the more exotic features of heroic mythology.

While it may be correct to see the *Iliad* as developing throughout the poet's career, and it is certain that many of the objections to Phoenix's presence are outweighed by the positive contribution his speech makes, it remains peculiar that the poet should have overlooked the cluster of duals in a short section of text. Nowhere else does Homer nod in quite so marked and localized a fashion: there is nothing quite so strange as the problem of the duals elsewhere in the epic. Perhaps this is one case in which 'analytic' arguments may still have some validity, but not when directed at the existence of Phoenix. Rather, we might turn the problem on its head and consider the possibility that the passage in which the embassy is despatched has been interfered with by some post-Homeric rhapsode. A possible motive might be the oddity of Phoenix being present in Agamemnon's camp: this was, perhaps, accepted casually by the main poet, but seemed anomalous to a successor, for is not Phoenix part of the entourage of Achilles? Like Patroclus, he should be attendant upon the hero, listening to the embassy, eventually goaded into utterance when he hears Achilles speaking so rashly and with such hostility. (His protests can in fact be seen as a less successful anticipation of Patroclus' appeal in book 16.[15]) If this hypothesis is correct, then the later poet would not be an interpolator but an imperfect editor, who, having decided that Phoenix ought to be in Achilles' camp already, changed Homer's plurals into duals accordingly, but overlooked the line in which Nestor appoints Phoenix as a member of the embassy (168) – the only line which makes it obvious that Phoenix is in Agamemnon's camp. It is easier still to suppose that he missed the later references to making up a bed for Phoenix (617–18, 620ff., 690). Problems, of course, remain, as with all discussion of this puzzling crux; but the false note is more plausibly ascribed to a later bard than to Homer himself.

Iliad 16. 777–800

So long as the sun was climbing still to the middle heaven,
so long the thrown weapons of both took hold, and men dropped under them;
but when the sun had gone to the time for unyoking of cattle,
then beyond their very destiny the Achaeans were stronger   780
and dragged the hero Cebriones from under the weapons
and the clamour of the Trojans, and stripped the armour from his shoulders.
And Patroclus charged with evil intention in on the Trojans.
Three times he charged in with the force of the running war god,
screaming a terrible cry, and three times he cut down nine men;   785
but as for the fourth time he swept in, like something greater
than human, there, Patroclus, the end of your life was shown forth,
since Phoebus came against you there in the strong encounter
dangerously, nor did Patroclus see him as he moved through
the battle, and shrouded in a deep mist came in against him   790
and stood behind him, and struck his back and his broad shoulders
with a flat stroke of the hand so that his eyes spun. Phoebus
Apollo now struck away from his head the helmet
four-horned and hollow-eyed, and under the feet of the horses
it rolled clattering, and the plumes above it were defiled   795
by blood and dust. Before this time it had not been permitted
to defile in the dust this great helmet crested in horse-hair;
rather it guarded the head and the gracious brow of a godlike
man, Achilles; but now Zeus gave it over to Hector
to wear on his head, Hector whose own death was close to him.   (Tr. R. Lattimore)

The description of the advancing day not only marks the passage of long hours of fighting, but also anticipates the downfall of Patroclus: the declining sun symbolizes the hero's decline in fortune.[16] More generally, we recall that this will mark the end of Hector's day of success (11. 191–4, p. 46 above). In this final moment of his *aristeia* Patroclus' prowess reaches supreme heights: his onslaught slays 27 men. Similarly the Achaeans are on the verge of achieving the impossible, contrary to what is destined (780). Their champion is described in godlike terms: 'with the force of the running war god' (784), 'like something greater than human' (786); but as always with such comparisons there is the implication that he remains less than a god.[17] The sequence 'thrice ... and then the fourth time' is ominous, regularly anticipating a change or reversal of fortune.

The way in which the poet addresses Patroclus (the device called 'apostrophe') his aroused much comment. The technique has already been used at earlier points in the book (lines 11, 584, 754, and esp. 692–3: 'whom first, whom last did you slay, Patroclus, when the gods summoned you to your death?'). In passages such as these the emotional involvement of the poet is exceptionally prominent. The use of the vocative may have originated as a metrical convenience, and in some cases elsewhere seems relatively colourless (esp. 15. 582), but the ancient commentators regarded it as a deliberately pathetic device, and most recent discussions agree.[18] The fact that Homer uses it most with sympathetic characters, especially Menelaus and Patroclus, supports this view.[19] It is poignant that the poet anticipates Patroclus' demise while speaking to his own character; the effect resembles the scenes in which Zeus, with similar detachment and compassion, speaks pityingly to mortals who cannot hear his words (esp. 17. 201–8, addressing Hector).

The intervention of Apollo is momentous but invisible to Patroclus: he comes upon his victim suddenly and violently, 'dangerously' (789: more literally, 'terrible'). Here again a stylistic device which often has little or no significance is deployed powerfully, with the adjective *deinos* held back to the beginning of line 789.[20] The actions of Apollo are described in a lengthy passage, extending beyond the section quoted: the effect is almost that of seeing a sequence of events in slow motion. Both the direct action of a god and the prolonged narration of the attack enhance Patroclus' status. The whole episode is unusual in that three agents are involved in Patroclus' death: Apollo stuns the victim and strips him of Achilles' armour, Euphorbus wounds him, Hector finishes him off.[21] The whole process from the beginning of this passage to the bold response of Hector to the dying man's words occupies nearly 100 lines. As elsewhere, the poet emphasizes important scenes by amplification and elaboration of detail.

The inner eye of the audience is directed not so much toward the bewildered Patroclus as to the armour falling from his body. This is the armour of Achilles, in which he had come forth to battle in the hope that the Trojans would be deceived. But Patroclus is an inadequate substitute for his friend, and the original arming scene in which he donned the greater man's armour is perhaps mirrored by the 'disarming' scene here, in which Patroclus is stripped of his defences. (It has also been suggested that the armour of Achilles may have been traditionally invulnerable, so that it must be removed before the wearer can be slain; if so, this is another case of Homer's preference for a less magical style of narrative.[22]) Divine armour befits a godlike hero: hence as long as Achilles wore this armour it was not fitting for it to be sullied by dirt and blood. The contrast between Patroclus and Achilles is emphasized again through the change in the condition of the helmet, now stained or 'defiled': the verb is tellingly repeated (795, 797). Glorious past is contrasted with ignominious present ('before this time . . . but now'); beauty and distinction are brought low, in both man and armour. Soon it will be Patroclus who is defiled in the dust. The final lines of the extract look to the future: Hector, favoured by Zeus, may now wear this helmet, but for a brief time only: his own death is near. The last line quoted above falls into two halves: the first completes the summing-up of Hector's triumph, the second shows us a glimpse of his future defeat, implicit in his victory.[23]

This last point is reinforced by Patroclus' dying words, close to the end of book 16 (852–4): 'You yourself are not one who will live long, but now already / death and powerful destiny are standing beside you, / to go down under the hands of Aiakos' great son, Achilles' (tr. Lattimore). When Homer comes to narrate the death of Hector and the dragging of his corpse, he is concerned to recall many aspects of Patroclus' death, and some of the same motifs of dust and defilement reappear. Especially close are 22. 401–4:

> A cloud of dust rose where Hector was dragged, his dark hair was falling
> about him, and all that head that was once so handsome was tumbled
> in the dust; but at this time Zeus gave him over
> to his enemies, to be defiled in the land of his fathers.
>
> (Lattimore, modified)[24]

In both cases, a hero who was once triumphant and magnificent is laid low; in both, beauty is marred by dust and dirt; in both, the all-embracing power of Zeus is at work. The verbal techniques through which Homer arouses pity for his characters are as vital as his unobtrusive but far-reaching control over the plot and thematic structure of his narrative.

Iliad 18. 15–37, 50–1

While he was pondering this in his mind and his heart, the son of proud Nestor came up close to him with his warm tears falling, and gave his painful message: 'Alas, son of warrior Peleus, there is terrible news for you to hear, which I wish had never happened. Patroclus lies dead, and they are fighting over his body. It is naked now – Hector of the glinting helmet has his armour.'

So he spoke, and the black cloud of sorrow enveloped Achilles. He took up the sooty dust in both his hands and poured it down over his head, spoiling his handsome face: and the black ashes settled all over his sweet-smelling tunic. And he lay there with his whole body sprawling in the dust, huge and hugely fallen, tearing at his hair and defiling it with his own hands. And the serving-women that Achilles and Patroclus had won in war shrieked aloud in their hearts' grief, and ran out to flock round the warrior Achilles: all of them beat their breasts with their hands, and the strength collapsed from their bodies. And to one side Antilochus mourned with his tears falling, and he held the hands of Achilles as his glorious heart groaned: he was afraid that Achilles might take a knife and cut his own throat. Achilles gave out a terrible cry, and his honoured mother heard him, where she sat by the side of her old father in the depths of the sea, and she wailed loud in response. And the goddesses gathered round her, all the daughters of Nereus ... The silvery cave filled with them; and they all beat their breasts together ... (tr. Hammond)

This is the most painful moment for Achilles in the entire poem – the moment in which he discovers that by persevering in his wrath and sending Patroclus out in his place he has doomed his beloved friend. The fact that Patroclus himself bears some responsibility, stressed in book 16 by the poet and briefly implied in Achilles' earlier speech of misgiving (12–14), is ignored in the flood of emotion which overwhelms the hero. From Antilochus' tears and from the opening words of his speech it is clear that he beings bad news, and he makes no effort to delay or conceal it. Achilles' failure to reply indicates the enormity of his grief: Homer here anticipates one of the dramatic devices of Greek tragedy, the momentous silence.[25]

This passage, and the scene which follows, form one of the chief examples put forward by critics practising what has been rather unsatisfactorily called 'neo-analysis'. The label associates this approach with the older methods of the analysts, but the similarity is not very great. Both schools have attempted to discern different layers or stages in the compositional process, but whereas the analysts normally tried to divide the poem into strata, the neo-analysts are concerned more with the influence of earlier versions on the surviving epics.[26] As for the passage quoted, it has been persuasively argued that the poet is deliberately composing this scene in such a way as to remind the audience of an epic narration of Achilles' own death. The most important points supporting this argument are: (a) the similarity of the expression in line 22 ('the black cloud of sorrow ...') to familiar formulae for death, combined with Achilles' prostrate position in the following lines; (b) the lamentation of Thetis and the Nereids, who are listed at considerable length: their intense grief would be appropriate for the death of Thetis' son, rather than the death of the mortal Patroclus; (c) the use of the phrase 'Thetis began the lament' (18. 51), language else-where applied to mourners over a dead man;[27] (d) the way in which Thetis cradles her son's head in her arms, a gesture associated with the mourner at a death-bed (18. 71, cf. 23. 136, 24. 724),[28] (e) the parallels between this scene and the detailed description of Achilles' funeral in the *Odyssey* (xxiv. 43 ff.). A particularly interesting parallel is the use of the phrase in 26, 'huge and hugely fallen', used in the same passage of the *Odyssey* of Achilles, and elsewhere only of another dead man, Cebriones (xxiv. 39 f., 16. 775 f.). All of these points seem to suggest that Achilles' death is fore-shadowed here: the reason is obvious, since the decision he is about to make will ensure the death which he has previously been able to avoid. Thetis' words as she prepares to join her son emphasize this inevitable outcome.

If these arguments are accepted, it follows that Achilles' death and funeral had been described in earlier epic, whether by the *Iliad*-poet him-self or by his predecessors. An important distinction needs to be made, however. The *Iliad* could be making conscious use of (and allusion to) earlier poetry without necessarily drawing on any of the specific epic poems about which we have evidence. The neo-analysts have often marred their case by insisting on the priority of a specific poem in the so-called Epic Cycle: in this case, it was often assumed that the poem which we know to have narrated the death of Achilles, namely the *Aethiopis*, was the 'source' for this passage of the *Iliad*. Sceptics can simply declare that the evidence suggests that the *Aethiopis* is in fact later than Homer, or may insist that the two poems are quite independent. It is preferable to leave the specific relationship between Homer and the Cycle out of the picture, and to think rather in terms of a tradition about the death of Achilles, which the *Iliad* presupposes and exploits. That tradition may well have included many of the elements mentioned by Proclus in his summary of the *Aethiopis*, but it is not necessary to assume that one poem is solely dependent on the other. The important point is that it seems likely that the simpler, more obvious use of these motifs – in a description of Thetis mourning for Achilles – came first, whereas the *Iliad*'s more subtle re-deployment of langauge and situation is a secondary development.[29] Like many other passages discussed in this Survey, the opening of book 18 effectively contradicts Erich Auerbach's famous account of Homer's narrative style, according to which everything is on the surface, and there is no room for complexity, mystery, or 'multilayeredness'.[30]

The role of Antilochus as messenger to Achilles is also of interest in this connection.[31] Even without neo-analytical theories it is clear that Antilochus, youthful son of Nestor, is a figure of some importance in the last six or eight books of the poem: he is one of the last to hear of Patroclus' death, Menelaus breaks the news to him in an emotional speech, he seems to be the obvious person to take the news to Achilles. Later he is prominent in the funeral games, a hot-headed competitor who nevertheless knows when to concede in the face of objections from his elders. Achilles seems to show him special favour; he smiles at Antilochus' enthusiastic protestation of his rights – the only place in the poem where Achilles does smile (23. 555–6). It is as though Achilles responds to Antilochus' impulsiveness: indeed, the latter's indignation at being deprived of his prize seems to be a small-scale parallel to the great wrath of Achilles (see esp. 1. 29 ~ 23. 553).[32] But whereas Agamemnon's grasping ill-will brought forth the momentous anger of Achilles, in book 23 Achilles is the generous peace maker, and both Menelaus' bad temper and Antilochus' pique are appeased.

It is not going too far to say that Antilochus is becoming almost a substitute for Patroclus – and in the last book of the *Odyssey* the two men are named together as part of Achilles' entourage in the underworld (xxiv. 16, cf. 77–9). Neo-analytic critics see this as having additional significance in view of the parallels between Patroclus' role in the *Iliad* and Antilochus' role in the *Aethiopis* and possibly in earlier versions of the same tale. Just as Hector killed Patroclus, so in the lost epic Memnon killed Antilochus; in both cases Achilles exacted revenge. Strictly speaking this is difficult to reconcile with the *Iliad*'s version, since we are told that Achilles' doom awaits him 'immediately after Hector', and at the end of the poem we assume that his death is imminent, at most a few days away. Here again it can be argued that the story-line of the *Iliad* is a later development, that Achilles' revenge on Hector is modelled on Achilles' revenge on Memnon, hard though it is for moderns to accept that so central a part of the plot should be derivative.[33] This argument may well be found less persuasive than the neoanalytic account of book 18, and its implications for our appreciation of the *Iliad* are less clear. Further explorations of Homer's 'sources', however fascinating, would take us into still more uncertain territory.

Odyssey 11. 543–67

Other souls of the dead and gone still stood there sorrowfully, each of them questioning me on whatever touched him most. Only the soul of Ajax the son of Telamon kept aloof, nursing anger still at my victory in the contest when beside the ships I made my claim for the armour of Achilles, whose goddess-mother offered the prize. Would I had never won that prize!

Because of it, the earth closed over heroic Ajax, who alike in presence and in prowess sur-
passed all other Danaans after the matchless son of Peleus. To him I now spoke appeasing
words:

'Ajax, son of the noble Telamon, is it then a thing beyond all hope that in death at least
you should set aside your wrath against me for the winning of those hateful arms? The prize
that the gods there offered was to bring distress on all the Argives when the tower of
strength that you had been was forever lost to them. Ever since you perished, our grief for
you has been like the grief for the son of Peleus, Achilles himself; and no other was the cause
of all this but Zeus; he it was who bore hate unbounded against the host of Achaean spears-
men, and because of that decreed your doom. Come to me now, Lord Ajax, and hear the
words that I wish to speak; conquer your spirit and pride of heart'.

So I spoke, but he made no answer to me, only followed to Erebus the other souls of men
dead and gone.

Then, despite his anger, he might still have spoken to me, or I to him, but my heart was
eager to see the souls of the other dead. (Tr. Shewring, with slight modifications)

In the land of the shades, far from normal human existence, Odysseus has
spoken with the ghosts of Agamemnon and Achilles. Other comrades flock
around him and speak with him; only Ajax stands aloof, unable to forget or
forgive his rival in the contest for Achilles' divine armour. Here Odysseus
tries to make amends, not without a few subtle touches of flattery: in particular, by declaring that 'our grief for you has been like the grief for the son
of Peleus.' Traditionally, in the *Odyssey* and elsewhere, Ajax is second-best
to Achilles.[34] Again, we should note the way in which Odysseus seeks to
slide responsibility for all the disastrous affair of the arms on to the gods
(558 ff. 'no other was the cause of all this but Zeus ...' Cf. 555). This
speech, like Priam's words to Helen in 3. 164, represents delicacy and tact,
not strict theological doctrine. Odysseus' tone is predominantly one of
compassion and regret, but he concludes by inviting Ajax to come closer
and listen to his story: as usual, he is eager to be the centre of attention. But
Ajax is not to be persuaded, and his silent, unreconciled withdrawal shows
us the kind of hero that he is: it expresses a kind of resolution and strength
which Odysseus will never have and perhaps does not want.

The lines which follow, however, may seem startling and incongruous.
'Then, despite his anger, he might still have spoken to me, or I to him, but
my heart was eager to see the souls of the other dead.' (565–7) Editors
since antiquity have cut out this conclusion to the episode, wishing to leave
Ajax's silent, disdainful exit unqualified. Surely, they argue, Ajax would not
have given in, and in any case what a shocking attitude for Odysseus to
adopt ('well, sorry Ajax, I really don't have the time ...').[35] But we must
remember that it is Odysseus who is telling the story at this point, and that
here as elsewhere in the first-person narrative he may be trying to put

himself in a good light. On this reading, the final comment can be seen as bravado on Odysseus' part. We know, and in his heart he knows, that he could never have prevailed on Ajax to give way: but he is not prepared to admit it to the admiring Phaeacian audience. 'Or I to him', an inappropriate alternative in the circumstances, is a stumbling give-away.[36]

This interpretation of the passage in question is reinforced by detailed study of the narrative technique of Odysseus' account of his own adventures, in an important paper by Irene de Jong.[37] Her essay establishes that the vocabulary and style of the hero's narrative differs from the normal manner of the poet, who narrates his tale in less emotional terms and with greater detachment. Thus Odysseus emphasizes the folly of his companions and his own quick wit, lays stress on the sufferings endured and the ingenuity with which they are surmounted; he is proud of his own foresight in bringing strong wine with him when exploring the Cyclops' territory; he makes sure that the audience do not miss the point about the size of the stag he slew and carried back to his camp (x. 168, 171, 180), or the magnitude of the terrible rock that closes off the cave of Polyphemus; and he singles out the loss of six companions to Scylla as 'the most pitiful thing that I saw' (xii. 258–9: see below). The technique heightens our involvement and establishes the emotional tone of the hero's narrative as distinct from that of the poet's own tale.

Odyssey 12. 244–59

We had looked that way [i.e. towards the whirlpool Charybdis] with the fear of death upon us; and at that moment Scylla snatched up from inside my ship the six of my crew who were strongest of arm and sturdiest. When I turned back my gaze to the ship in search of my companions, I saw only their feet and hands as they were lifted up; they were calling out to me in their heart's anguish, crying out my name for the last time. As when a fisherman on a promontory takes a long rod to snare little fishes with his bait and casts his ox-hair line down into the sea below, then seizes the creatures one by one and throws them ashore still writhing; so Scylla swung my writhing companions up to the rocks, and there at the entrance began devouring them as they shrieked and held out their hands to me in their extreme of agony. Many pitiful things have met my eyes in my toilings and searchings through the sea-paths, but this was the most pitiful of all. (Tr. Shewring)

Scylla, the hideous sea-monster with six heads on long necks, immortal and invulnerable, was described in horrific terms by Circe earlier in the book (xii. 85–100), where Odysseus was warned that he could not hope to evade her entirely, but must content himself with losing no more than six men. This inhuman being combines the terrors of nightmares with the tall stories of seafarers: few passages in the poem have a more spine-chilling effect. Odysseus' narration lays stress on the pain he feels at the loss of his comrades: as elsewhere, it is made clear that his homecoming, though in the end successful, involves suffering and loss. The episode is also used to show Odysseus' continuing efforts to deal with the weird world of the wanderings in conventional heroic terms: despite Circe's warnings that any such attempt is futile, he hopes to repel Scylla, and dons his 'glorious armour' in preparation for her assault. In fact, not only does he fail even to see her sudden attack, but he could not slay her if he tried: 'Scylla is not of mortal kind, she is a deathless monster, grim and baleful, savage, not to be wrestled with.' (Circe's words again, 118 f.) He admits in retrospect that he forgot Circe's advice; but to ignore divine warnings can lead to disaster, as we see again when his companions kill the cattle of the sun. There is a double lesson here for Odysseus: he must be prepared to follow the instructions of the gods (as he follows Athena's in the second half), and he must also recognize that in some circumstances the old heroic ethic of confronting one's enemy in open combat is ineffective. In one respect, however, he already possesses some of the skills he will need in future: he can keep his own counsel. In giving directions to his men earlier 'I had stopped short of mentioning Scylla, an inexorable horror: the crew in fear might have left their oars and have huddled down in the hold' (xii. 223–5). Secrecy and self-restraint will be the keynotes of his behaviour in the Ithacan narrative which is to follow.

Perhaps the most striking aspect of the passage quoted is the simile comparing Scylla to a fisherman drawing in his catch. Like many similes which are applied to supernatural beings, it makes an extraordinary event more vivid and imaginable.[38] More important, it does so by a kind of inversion of normality: whereas the poet and his audience are familiar with the sight of a man catching fish, Odysseus witnesses a creature of the sea 'catching' men. In the strange and remote world of the wanderings, man is confronted by impossible beings in unnatural settings: heroic valour, as we have seen, is futile against natural force or immortal monster.[39] Similarly on land the gigantic Laestrygonians are seen spearing men as if they were fish (x. 124). Another parallel comes in book v, where the poet is recounting Odysseus' storm-tossed journey from Calypso's island: 'as when many pebbles stick to the suckers of an octopus when he is dragged out of his lair, so the skin was stripped off his [Odysseus'] hands against the rocks' (v. 432–5).[40] There Odysseus, out of his element, is helpless and injured whereas the sea-creature is not. Another common feature in the fisherman-simile is that it describes something everyday, a timeless scene involving an ordinary man rather than a hero (and indeed the heroes generally do not eat fish except in extreme circumstances).[41] The ordeal of the epic hero is contrasted with the simplicity and order of 'normal' life; at the same time, similes like this also sometimes serve to remind us of the very humanity of the heroes.

The simile in this extract has a further parallel –possibly even a counterpart – in a much later passage, where Odysseus stands triumphantly in his own palace, with the suitors lying dead before him.

He saw the suitors, one and all, lying huddled in blood and dust. They were like the fish that fishermen with their close-meshed nets have drawn out from the whitening sea on to the curving beach; they are all heaped upon the sand, longing for the sea waves, but the sun beats down and takes their lives. So did the suitors lie in heaps, one upon another.

(xxii. 383–9, tr. Shewring)

With Odysseus back in his own rightful place, the 'natural' order is re-established, and the man becomes the fisherman.[42]

There is certainly similarity of subject, but does this count as an echo? As we have seen, much recent criticism of Homer has found extensive cross-reference and interconnection between different parts of the poems, often convincingly; similar attention has been focussed on the similes, with rather less success. 'Linked' similes certainly exist, but are perhaps most persuasively identified when they occur in swift succession.[43] Thus in *Iliad* 2, three similes are used to describe the motion of the Achaean army in terms of the movement of the sea (144–6, 209–10, 394–7); it is not necessary, but certainly possible, to see these as planned in a sequence. In book xvi of the *Odyssey*, we first find Eumaeus' joy at the safe return of Telemachus compared with that of a father tearfully welcoming home his son after many years (this while the true father, Odysseus, is present in disguise). Shortly afterwards, when Odysseus has revealed himself, father and son weep together, and another simile compares them with birds who have lost their young unfledged (xvi. 14–21, 216–19). There is a thematic analogy, but the passages seem too different in subject to speak of a close connection. Other suggestions, however ingenious, are often very implausible. But the possibility of very long-range 'linking' of similes can hardly be denied in view of the famous case describing Odysseus' and Penelope's reunion (xxiii. 231–40, quoted on p. 72 above), which recalls the actual experiences of Odysseus in book v and seems also to pick up the themes of a simile there (v. 394–9).[44] None of these cases, however, demands actual knowledge of the other passage, and there is never an explicit cross-reference; consequently, it may be better to speak in terms of recurring subject-matter or thematic concerns. At a minimum, however, Homer often shapes his similes for more than mere ornamentation, and linguistic study has suggested that here at least we may see the hand of the individual poet at work, rather than the stock material of the tradition.[45]

Odyssey 14. 196 ff. (extracts)

I might well enough spend a year recounting the sorrows of my spirit and still not come to an end of them – all the sorrows that I have toiled through because the gods willed it so. Wide Crete is the home I boast of, and I was a rich man's son. He had many other sons as well, bred in the house and born in wedlock. My own mother was a concubine, bought as a slave; yet I, no less than the true-born sons, was given regard by my father, Castor son of Hylax . . . But the death-spirits carried him down to Hades' home, and his haughty sons divided his substance up, casting lots for it. To me they gave a house and very little besides, but by my own merits I won for wife a daughter of very wealthy parents, because I was no fool and no coward . . . Work on the land I was never fond of, or such care of the household as brings up children in prosperity. The things that I loved were ships and oars and battles and gleaming spears . . . Even before the sons of the Achaeans ever set foot on the land of Troy, I had nine times had under my command men and swift ships to sail against foreign shores, and hence much booty reached my hands . . . the people began to urge myself and Idomeneus to lead an expedition of ships to the war at Troy. To deny what they asked was not possible., the people's voice was too compelling . . . [and after the Trojan war] for a month, no more, I stayed at home and enjoyed myself there with my children and my wedded wife and my possessions; then impulse urged me to fit out vessels and sail to Egypt with my heroic comrades . . . [but after his comrades recklessly raided Egyptian farms] the Egyptians killed many of us with the keen bronze; others they took inland alive to labour for them in slavery . . . I dashed the wrought helmet from my head, I threw down the shield from my shoulder, the spear from my hand; I ran to meet the king's chariot and I touched and kissed his knees. He had compassion, and rescued me, gave me a place in his own chariot and took me in tears back to his palace, fearing the wrath of Zeus who protects strangers . . . In that place I stayed for seven years, and I gathered much wealth among the men of Egypt, because they all made me gifts. But when the eighth year came, there came with it a cunning-witted Phoenician, a rogue who had done harm enough in the world already. He won me over with his craftiness and took me away with him to Phoenicia . . . then he put me aboard a ship that would sail the sea to Libya. His plan in this was a treacherous one; I was to help him to take the cargo there, but he hoped to sell me myself and get a huge price for me. Though I had misgivings, I had no choice but to go aboard with him . . . etc. etc. (tr. Shewring)

This is enough to give the flavour of Odysseus' longest lying narrative, the tale he spins to the loyal swineherd, who listens with fascination (see 361–2 and xvii. 518–21).[46] It is superfluous to comment on the hero's marvellous fluency in invention, but we may note that none of the yarns he spins is precisely the same, though there are common elements. In his lies he regularly portrays himself as a Cretan, and it is tempting to think of the saying 'all Cretans are liars', though that may itself arise partly from the stories in the *Odyssey*! He clearly suits his tale to his addressee: Eumaeus too was carried away by villainous Phoenicians and sold as a slave, as we learn when he recounts his life-story in book xv (351ff. esp. 415–84). It is natural to suppose that Odysseus really knows this already,[47] and indeed he draws a comparison later between Eumaeus' experiences and his own tale.

This speech can be studied in various ways. One procedure, now out of favour, is to try to reconstruct from the lies the 'real' adventures of Odysseus or of some real person on whom he is based; more plausibly, some have argued that parts of the lies preserve valuable clues to other, probably older poetic versions of the travels of Odysseus.[48] A more fruitful method is to study the thematic material, comparing the other lies and the rest of the poem's narrative.[49] What emerges is that a great deal of the speech consists of elements redeployed in various contexts: thus the disastrous raid on the Egyptians resembles the raid by Odysseus' men on the Cicones, the first of his adventures after leaving Troy, and the seven-year stay in Egypt is paralleled by Menelaus' sojourn in the same country. We see also that Odysseus here, as in the longer narrative to the Phaeacians, takes care to build up his own image: he is a fearless and inexhaustible fighter, ever game for adventure; it was his comrades who behaved foolishly in the Egyptian episode and who then panicked, whereas he had the initiative to throw himself on the king's mercy; he is quick-witted enough to suspect the Phoenician's motives, and so forth. The ethical outlook of the false tale also corresponds to that of the *Odyssey* as a whole: compassion and respect for suppliants or strangers are admirable qualities (as the honourable actions of the king of Egypt show); gathering gifts and booty, if it can be done safely, is always desirable; and violent action is not the answer to everything, so that one must sometimes cut one's losses and live to fight another day. In the lies as in the main plot, Odysseus is a survivor.

Finally, there is the historical dimension of the lies, and of the *Odyssey* more generally. We can take it for granted that no wandering sailor ever encountered a Cyclops or visited the land of the dead, but in the lies which Odysseus narrates there is nothing physically impossible or intrinsically improbable. We are not here concerned to recover the actual experiences of a traveller, but to gain some idea of what Homer's audience thought of as 'typical' of sea-voyaging and adventures abroad. Even here we should make some allowance for epic amplification: it is perhaps unlikely that a single leader made nine successful raids, and we may feel sure that an invader turned suppliant would have been speared by subordinates before he got anywhere near the physical person of the king of Egypt. Yet many elements of Odysseus' narrative seem entirely realistic: the bastard son of a rich man, favoured by his father but treated less well by the legitimate sons; disgruntlement over inheritance (we naturally think of Hesiod); the bold entrepreneur, scorning the easier life at home and loving the excitement of sea-travel.[50] Thucydides remarked on the way in which Homer treats piracy and looting as normal, almost a familiar profession and certainly not something to which a man might be ashamed to admit (Thuc. 1. 5): this was characteristic, as he deduced, of the unstable and warlike conditions of earlier times. Kidnapping and abduction went along with looting, as Herodotus' opening chapters also imply (1. 1–4, cf. Eumaeus' tale, xv. 425 ff., 449 ff.). But it was not only looting which might take a man abroad: the Phoenician trader is sailing all the way to Libya with his unnamed cargo, and Athena, seeking a plausible excuse for her disguised appearance in Ithaca, adopts the identity of Mentes from Taphos, carrying a cargo of iron to the city of Temese which he wishes to exchange for copper.[51] Herodotus mentions a real-life equivalent, the Samian merchant Kolaios, a figure of the mid-600s, who was on his way to Egypt when he was carried off course by storms and ended up in Tartessos, north of Cadiz (Hdt. 4. 152).[52] He was renowned as the richest merchant of his time. Trading is normal, though there are signs elsewhere that it is not quite the done thing for an aristocrat (viii. 159–64). The knowledge in our passage of Egypt and the Nile also anticipates historically attested campaigns: surviving graffiti carved on the colossal statue of Rameses II at Abu Simbel show that Greek mercenaries were in service to the Egyptian king Psammetichus II around 600 B.C.[53]

The *Odyssey* thus yields much evidence to the social historian, provided it is recognized that epic narrative needs to be handled with some care. Another aspect is the Greek expansion overseas, as population growth, social dissension or trading aspirations drove the various communities to establish colonies in far-flung areas of the Mediterranean.[54] According to tradition the process began in Sicily, with Naxos colonized from Euboean Chalcis, and Syracuse from Corinth in about 735, probably within a generation of the *Odyssey*-poet's lifetime. It is remarkable that Alcinous assures Odysseus that his people's ships can transport him home with ease, 'even if it is very much further away than Euboea' (vii. 321).[55] Echoes of this movement have been detected elsewhere. In book ix, Odysseus' description of the island off the Cyclopes' coast gives a strong impression of an opportunity missed: it has woods, vines, arable land, a good harbour, 'but the Cyclopes have no red-cheeked ships, or shipwrights' (*Od.* ix. 116–41). Here as in other respects the Cyclopes are defined in opposition to mankind, as primitive and antisocial, unpolitical beings.[56] The opening of book vi, which describes how Alcinous' father moved to Scheria in order to escape the maraudings of other Cyclopes, lays down the minimal formula for establishing a colony: 'he ringed the city with a wall, built houses, gave the gods temples, apportioned land for tillage' (vi. 7–10). Later in the same book the city is described at greater length by Nausicaa (262–9); it is clearly a Greek-style *polis*. The same may be confidently assumed of the community surrounding Odysseus' palace on Ithaca, and is probable even of Troy: arguments that Homer portrays some form of pre-polis society are difficult to sustain.[57] Reverting to the passage under discussion, a final point which points towards future political developments occurs in the lines which speak of 'the people's voice', the *dēmou phēmis*, as putting pressure on Idomeneus and others to marshall a force against Troy.[58] Kings and nobles make the decisions, but the people have some influence on their deliberations. This balance of political forces is in accord with the 'merito-cratic' air of a society in which a bastard son (admittedly, son of an eminent man, like Archilochus of Paros) with a small inheritance can make a good marriage and rise to wealth and fortune.[59] Archilochus too was a survivor, prepared to drop his shield and fight another day.[60]

Odysseus' account of his expedition to Egypt, his subsequent tale of how he escaped from the Phoenician, are a world away from the isle of Calypso and the rock of six-headed Scylla. While they cannot be safely trawled for historical dates and facts, the 'lies' shed indirect light on attitudes, values, expectations. Something of the pessimistic tone of an authentic beggar sustains the sober morality found elsewhere in the *Odyssey*, with its emphasis on the instability of fortune and the blindness of men to the future.[61] But there is also a note of exuberance and confidence, which reminds the reader that life is exhilarating, the world large and full of new surprises, new experiences. It is not too imaginative to see here a reflection of the spirit of some of the Greek settlers and travellers as they set out to explore, sometimes to exploit, the Mediterranean and beyond. Theirs was a simpler world. Yet we can still enjoy and learn from Homer's vision of the greatness, the baseness, the hopes, and the follies of mankind.

NOTES

1. Cf. Hdt. 2. 113–20, esp. 120. 1–2, for scepticism; for disapproval, see Alcaeus 42, 283 Lobel-Page; Aesch. *Agam.* 62, 225, 448, 681 ff., Eur. *Androm.* 590–69, *Iph. Taur.* 356, 438 ff., *Cyclops* 179 ff. (!), etc.

2. On Helen see also K. J. Reckford, 'Helen in the *Iliad*', *GRBS* 5 (1964), 5–20; Kakridis 1971, 25–53; Reichel 1994, 264–71 (with bibl.). On this episode see O. Lendle, 'Paris, Helena und Aphrodite. Zur Interpretation des 3. Gesanges der Ilias', *A&A* 14 (1968), 63–71.

3. See e.g. the notes in J. T. Hooker's and M. M. Willcock's commentaries on the scene; also the older edition by W. Leaf. Kirk 1985 sits on the fence.

4. A point stressed by Kirk 1985 ad loc. Almost identical lines are found at 4. 208, 11. 804, 13. 468; compare also 2. 142, 14. 459, 17. 123.

5. Kullmann 1960, 250f., who regards the scene as indebted to the Cyclic poem the *Cypria*; cf. e.g. Edwards 1987, 196.

6. In 445 it is unclear whether κραναῇ is a proper name (as we might speak of the island of Rockall) or an adjective. Even if the former is right, the name suggests the discomfort of the lovers.

7. Cf. Macleod 1983, 10.

8. See esp. Kakridis 1971, 68–75; also Griffin 1980, 6–8.

9. On Phoenix's speech see further Lohmann 1970, 245–76; Rosner 1976, R. Scodel, 'The autobiography of Phoenix: *Iliad* 9. 444–95', *AJP* 103 (1982), 128–36. On the Meleager-paradigm see p. 7.

10. Macleod 1982, 34.

11. For obvious reasons, translations often gloss over this, translating the duals as plurals: e.g. Hammond's Penguin. Fitzgerald even inserts at 182 '*Following Phoenix*, Aias and Odysseus walked together ...'! Exceptions include Lattimore and Fagles.

12. For a fuller account of the difficulties see Hainsworth 1993, 57, 85–7; Griffin 1995, 51–3. In English the major analytic discussion is Page 1959, 298ff. For subsequent argument see D. Motzkus, *Untersuchungen zum 9. Buch der Ilias* (diss. Hamburg, 1964), C. Segal, 'The embassy and the duals of *Iliad* 9. 182–89', *GRBS* 9 (1968), 101–14 (unpersuasive), W. S. Wyatt, 'The embassy and the duals in *Iliad* 9', *AJP* 106 (1985), 399–408; Edwards 1987, 218–19, 228–30.

13. Reinhardt 1961, 212–42, endorsed by Hainsworth 1993, 57.

14. A phrase used by Willcock 1976, 99, and by Hainsworth (cited in last n.).

15. E.g. Edwards 1987, 228, on whose discussion I am building here.

16. See further Fenik 1968, 216, Willcock 1976, 126 and 189, Taplin 1992, 156.

17. Cf. Griffin 1980, ch. 3.

18. For the scholia see Richardson 1980, 272. For modern discussion see e.g. A. Parry 1972, 8–22 = Parry 1989, 310–25; Janko on 13. 602–3.

19. In the *Odyssey* the situation is less clear: there the device is exclusively reserved for the swineherd Eumaeus.

20. For scepticism about the significance of this kind of placing of words, see S. E. Bassett, 'The so-called emphatic position of the runover word', *TAPA* 57 (1926), 116–48; M. W. Edwards, 'Some features of Homeric craftsmanship', *TAPA* 97 (1966), 139f.; contrast Tsagarakis 1982, 10–31; a thorough investigation of the question by C. Higbie, *Measure and music: enjambement and sentence structure in the Iliad* (Oxford, 1990).

21. Janko 1992, 408–10 explains this in neo-analytical terms, according to which the episode is modelled on the death of Achilles.

22. P. J. Kakridis, 'Achilles' Rüstung', *Hermes* 89 (1961), 288–97. The situation in the *Iliad* is complicated by the fact that Achilles at different stages has two separate sets of divine armour, the first being seized by Hector. See further Janko on 16. 130–54.

23. Compare the comment by J. Griffin, in his contribution to the joint article by Griffin and M. Hammond, 'Critical Appreciations VI: Homer, *Iliad* 1. 1–52', *G&R* 29 (1982), 126–42, at 142 n. 17: '"Half-lines in Homer" is a less obvious title than "Half-lines in Virgil", but it might make an interesting study.'

24. Also relevant are 16. 638–40, 17. 51–2, 439–40. Cf. Fenik 1968, 163, Segal 1971, 41–2, Griffin 1980, 134–8.

25. Cf. esp. Achilles himself in Aeschylus' *Myrmidons*, as shown by Ar. *Frogs* 832ff. and scholia, with O. Taplin, 'Aeschylean silences and silences in Aeschylus', *HSCP* 76 (1972), 57–97. For other cases see Richardson on *Hymn to Demeter* 197–201; cf. Richardson 1980, 281; I. de Jong, 'Silent characters in the *Iliad*', in Bremer et al. 1987, 105–21.

26. Fundamental treatment by Kakridis 1949, esp. 65–95; the authoritative collection of material is Kullmann 1960. More recent discussions include W. Kullmann, 'Oral poetry theory and neoanalysis in Homeric research', *GRBS* 25 (1984), 307–23, reprinted with other papers in Kullmann, *Homerische Motive* (Stuttgart, 1992); see also Edwards 1991, 15–19. Clark 1986 provides a bibliographical survey. Much of Malcolm Willcock's work on Homer is indebted to this school; I am grateful to him for sending me an essay on the whole subject forthcoming in a Leiden Companion to Homer.

27. See 18. 316 = 23. 17 (Achilles over Patroclus), 24. 723, 747, 761 (the women at Hector's funeral).

28. Kakridis 1949, 65f.; illustration in Vermeule 1979, 15.

29. Similar argument in Seaford 1994, 154–9, with criticism of the sceptics.

30. Auerbach's essay 'Odysseus' scar', the first chapter in his *Mimesis* (Berne, 1946; Eng. tr. 1953), has often been reprinted. For criticism see A. Köhnken, 'Die Narbe des Odysseus', *A&A* 22 (1976), 101–114 = Latacz 1991b, 491–513; de Jong 1987, 22–3, Lynn-George 1988, 2–27.

31. See further M. M. Willcock, 'The funeral games of Patroclus', *BICS* 20 (1973), 1–11 and 'Antilochus in the *Iliad*', in *Mélanges E. Delebecque* (Aix-en-Provence, 1983) 479–85.

32. Macleod 1982, 28–32, esp. 30.

33. See further Kullmann 1960, 37–8, 311, Seaford 1994, 154–6.

34. Cf. 470, 550–1, Soph. *Ajax* 1340f., *PMG* 898. Similarly in the games of *Iliad* 23, Ajax enters three contests and comes first in none of them.

35. See e.g. Page 1955, 26–7.

36. So esp. Eisenberger 1973, 184 (independently e.g. A. Parry, *Logos and Ergon in Thucydides* (N.Y., 1981), 29), endorsed by de Jong (see next n.), 5 and Sourvinou-Inwood 1995, 85.

37. I. J. F. de Jong, 'The Subjective Style in Odysseus' Wanderings', *CQ* 42 (1992), 1–11 (cf. already W. Suerbaum, 'Die Ich-Erzählungen des Odysseus', *Poetica* 2 (1968), 150–77). See also Rutherford 1986, 150 n. 33.

38. For fuller discussion of Homer's similes see H. Fränkel, *Die Homerischen Gleichnisse* (Göttingen, 1921); M. Coffey, 'The function of the Homeric simile', *AJP* 78 (1957), 113–32; W. C. Scott, *The oral nature of the Homeric simile* (Mnemos. Suppl. 58, Leiden, 1974) (with full lists); Moulton 1977, Macleod 1982, 48–50, Edwards 1987, ch. 12 and 1991, 24–41, Rutherford 1992, 73–7.

39. Cf. and contrast Kirk 1970, 162–71, who interprets the Cyclops myth along structuralist lines as a nature vs. culture story: primitive man-eating monster vs. shrewd intelligent human armed with a quick wit, wine, and fire. Note also the similes at ix. 384ff., 391ff., both applied to Odysseus as he proceeds with the perilous act of blinding the Cyclops. Both describe his action in terms of human craftsmanship: ship-building and the work of a bronzesmith, techniques of a civilized society.

40. Cf. Macleod 1982, 49.

41. See Griffin 1980, 19 on heroic diet: add Pl. *Rep.* 404b and context; Richardson 1975, 73 n. 6.

42. For other reversals, see Rutherford on xx. 356–7, and 1986, 152 n. 40.

43. See further Moulton 1977, ch. 1 and pp. 133–9 (sometimes over-subtle).

44. Moulton 1977, 128–9.

45. G. P. Shipp, *Studies in the Language of Homer* (Cambridge, 1953; 2nd edn. 1972), 208–22, argues on linguistic grounds that the elaborated similes are late in date, and this has been generally accepted (see e.g. Janko 1992, 12 [though ctr. his p. 9]). It is striking, in a poem so rich in formulaic material, that similes are so rarely repeated, even when the same subject matter is involved. Is this a sign of Homer's relative independence of the tradition?

46. For bibliography on the lies see ch. 3 n. 9 above.

47. For a different view see Stewart 1976, 90–1.

48. The first approach is pursued with perverse determination by Woodhouse 1930, esp. chh. 17–18; for emphatic rejection see Fenik 1974, 171 n. 69. The second, which concentrates especially on Odysseus' account of his experiences in Thesprotia, is expounded by S. West, 'An Alternative Nostos for Odysseus', *LCM* 6 (1981), 169–75.

49. Here the work of Fenik 1974, 167–71 is virtually definitive.

50. Cf. N. Purcell, 'Mobility and the Polis', in O. Murray-S. Price (edd.), *The Greek City from Homer to Alexander* (Oxford, 1990), 29–58, who touches on Homeric matters only in passing, but presents a stimulating picture of the Mediterranean background. See also H. Strasburger, 'Der soziologische Aspekt der homerischen Epen', *Gymn.* 60 (1953), 97–114, repr. in Strasburger, *Studien zur alten Geschichte* (Hildesheim, 1982) i. 491–518.

51. Both these places are hard to locate with any certainty: see S. West on i. 105 and 184.

52. See Boardman 1980, 114; M. Torelli, 'Il santuario di Hera a Gravisca', *PP* 26 (1971), 44–67.

53. R. Meiggs-D. Lewis, *A Selection of Greek Historical Inscriptions* (Oxford, 1969, rev. 1988), no. 7; Boardman 1980, 115–16, with illustrations.

54. H. Schaefer, 'Eigenart und Wesenszüge der griechischen Kolonisation', *Heidelberger Jahrbücher* 4 (1960), 77–93; A. J. Graham, *Colony and Mother City in Ancient Greece* (Manchester, 1964); id., *CAH* iii² 3. 163–95; Boardman 1980 (much-expanded revision of a 1964 book); many of the topics discussed there are developed further in J. Boardman, *The Diffusion of Classical Art in Antiquity* (London and Princeton, 1994). For a briefer treatment see L. H. Jeffery, *Archaic Greece: the City-States* (London, 1976), 50–7.

55. Interpretations of this reference vary: Garvie 1994 ad loc. suggests that 'to an Ionian poet

Euboea itself seemed to be on the western edge of the known world, so that Scheria must be an unimaginable distance beyond it.' M. L. West 1988, 172, argues that the *Odyssey* may itself have been composed in Euboea.

56. Cf. Vidal-Naquet 1970, rev. 1981, 84, 85–7.

57. Extended argument and bibliography on this debate in Raaflaub 1993. Seaford 1994, chh. 1–2 argues that the *polis* is emergent in Homer, but still weaker and less important than the *oikos*. The subject is also treated by S. R. Scully, *Homer and the Sacred City* (Cornell, 1990) (somewhat diffuse).

58. See further Raaflaub 1993, 54–9. On the use of the term *dēmos* in archaic Greece see e.g. W. Donlan, 'Changes and shifts in the meaning of Demos . . .' *PP* 25 (1970), 381–95. We may note incidentally that here, as in the *Iliad*, there is no trace of the more romantic notion that the Greek leaders, who had all been suitors of Helen, were now bound by an oath to aid her wronged husband. See Taplin 1990, 68–9, who argues that the three possible hints of this oath in the *Iliad* are not significant.

59. For a short but lively account of Archilochus' career and poetry see Jeffery (n. 54 above) 181–3; more detail on history in A. J. Graham, 'The Foundation of Thasos', *BSA* 73 (1978), 61–98; on poetry in A. P. Burnett, *Three Archaic Poets* (London, 1983), part 1.

60. Fr. 5 West, cf. fr. 114 on the right sort of general.

61. See e.g. in this speech xiv. 198, 213–5, 235–6, 243, 274–5, 310, 338. Elsewhere see esp. xviii. 130–50 (Odysseus to Amphinomus); also e.g. xix. 325–34, xx. 194 ff.

BIBLIOGRAPHICAL NOTE

Texts
The text most widely used is the Oxford Classical Text (Monro-Allen for the *Iliad*, Allen for the *Odyssey*), but it is widely agreed that this is deficient. G. Pasquali, *Storia della tradizione e critica del testo* (2nd edn., Florence, 1952) refuted Allen's classification of mss. into 'families'; N. Tachinoslis, *Handschriften und Ausgaben der Odyssee* (Frankfurt, 1984) showed the inaccuracy of his statements about their readings. See also R. Janko, 'The *Iliad* and its Editors: Dictation and Redaction', *ClAntiq.* 9 (1990), 324–34, N. G. Wilson, *PBA* 76 (1990), 316. For the *Odyssey* there is P. von der Mühll's edition (Basel, 1945) and now that of H. van Thiel (Hildesheim, 1991), with introd. in both German and English; the latter also promises an edition of the *Iliad*.

Commentaries
The most important change in the period since J. B. Hainsworth's 1969 survey is that we now have modern commentaries on the whole of Homer's text. Previous work, some of it now almost a century old, retains some value (esp. W. Leaf on the *Iliad*, 1900–2, for his clarity of presentation and firm grammatical grasp; also W. B. Stanford on the *Odyssey*, 1959, a sympathetic work though often very brief and selective in annotation); but the new Cambridge *Iliad* and the Oxford *Odyssey* must now be regarded as standard. For students a good reading text is M. M. Willcock's two-volume *Iliad* (Basingstoke, 1978–84). In addition, the special merits of C. W. Macleod's edition of *Iliad* 24 (Cambridge, 1982), with its long and sensitive introduction dealing with the poem as a whole, are well known. On a similar scale is J. Griffin's new edition of *Iliad* 9 (Oxford, 1995). Some brief notes on the larger new commentaries may be found useful.

The *Iliad* commentary is distinguished by its fine introductory essays, and it has been suggested that a list of these would be helpful to students.

Vol. 1 (Kirk 1985): The methods and aims of the commentary; The making of the *Iliad*, preliminary considerations; The structural elements of Homeric verse; Aristarchus and the scholia; The first four books of the *Iliad* in context.

(Note also the long general treatment of the Catalogue of Ships, effectively an independent essay.)

Vol. 2 (Kirk 1990): The Homeric gods: prior considerations [covers oriental influence and cultic 'realities']; Typical motifs and themes; The speech-element in the *Iliad*; History and fiction in the *Iliad*.

Vol. 3 (Hainsworth 1993): Formulas [a long and authoritative treatment]; The *Iliad* as Heroic Poetry.

Vol. 4 (Janko 1992): The gods in Homer: further considerations; The origins and evolution of the epic diction; The text and transmission of the *Iliad*.

Vol. 5 (Edwards 1991): The narrator and the audience; Composition by Theme; Similes; Style.

Vol. 6 (Richardson 1993): Structure and themes; Two special problems (book division and the end of the *Iliad* in relation to the *Odyssey*); Homer and his ancient critics.

In addition, all but the first volume provides at least brief introductions to each book (in vol. 1 the final part of the introduction serves this purpose). The final volume has a consolidated index of Greek words, but not of other topics. It would be otiose to say much about the relative merits of the various volumes, when such riches are presented in each; I merely note my agreement with those reviewers who find Janko's volume particularly acute and independent, while Edwards perhaps holds the balance most admirably between technical observation and literary sensitivity.

In general the *Odyssey* commentary is less successful and less well integrated. There are general essays of the kind described above only in vol. 1 (A. Heubeck, 'General Introduction', J. B. Hainsworth, 'The Epic Dialect', and S. West, 'The Transmission of the Text' – all, as one would expect, of high quality). Volume 2, by A. Heubeck and A. Hoekstra, includes a short introduction to the wanderings by the former, and an essay by the latter mainly concerned with the poetic dialect. In volume 3, J. Russo gives a general inroduction to books 17–20, and the other contributors (M. Fernandez-Galiano and A. Heubeck) provide short introductions to each of the last four books. Constraints of space are more of a problem: none of the contributors has as much as half the space devoted to four books of the *Iliad* (granted, the *Odyssey* is a shorter work), and Hainsworth and Russo in particular seem to suffer from this limitation (in view of this, the less advanced but longer treatments of some of these books by Garvie and myself may be useful alongside this work). There is also less cross-referencing and editorial coordination in the project. The effect is peculiar when one passes from Fernandez-Galiano's account of books 21–22 (severely analyst in tendency) to that of Heubeck on 23–24 (unitarian to a fault), and although commentators must of course be allowed to express their views, there is in this case insufficient space given to contrary opinions. It must be stressed again, however, that this is criticism of a work which despite deficiencies towers above anything else that has been done. The final volume includes cumulative indexes both of words and of subjects. For all of this devoted work generations of scholars and students will be grateful.

Translations
Translations of Homer become ever more numerous and, with the decline in wide knowledge of Greek, more important. Alexander Pope's versions, edited by Maynard Mack in volumes 7–10 of the Twickenham Pope edition, are dazzling and rhetorical, best read alongside a more faithful version. Those by Lang, Leaf and Myers (*Iliad*) and by Butcher and Lang (*Odyssey*), which adopted an archaic prose style in imitation of the King James Bible, are now probably hard to enjoy reading, though they have a certain dignity. Equally archaic though less distinguished are the old Loeb editions by A. T. Murray: his *Odyssey* has now been modernized by G. E. Dimock, and presumably something similar is planned for the *Iliad*. The old Penguin Classics by E. V. Rieu were enormously popular but excessively informal: his *Odyssey* has been revised and on the whole improved by Peter Jones (1991), and the *Iliad* completely replaced by M. Hammond (1987, an admirable prose version). An excellent prose *Odyssey* is the rendering by W. Shewring (Oxford, 1980). The most widely used verse translation is by Richmond Lattimore (*Iliad* 1951, *Odyssey* 1965), using a long line which approximates to the rhythm of the hexameter, and translating accurately but sometimes awkwardly. Other modern verse translations include those by Robert Fitzgerald (*Odyssey* 1961, *Iliad* 1974) and Robert Fagles (*Iliad* 1990). Christopher Logue's *Patrocleia* (London, 1962) was the first and be   of a series of very bold adaptations of parts of the *Iliad* into free verse in a modern and cynical mode; while sometimes brilliant, they

have also been much criticized (Ezra Pound's adaptations of Propertius are in some ways a parallel case).

The Oxford Book of Greek Verse in Translation, ed. T. E. Higham and C. M. Bowra (Oxford, 1938) contains renderings of 56 memorable passages by various translators, and an essay by Higham on the challenge facing the translator of Greek poetry. See now also The Oxford Book of Classical Verse in Translation, ed. A. Poole and J. Maule (1995).

Matthew Arnold's classic essay 'On Translating Homer', originally published in 1861 and often reprinted, is still well worth reading. More recent discussions of the problems include: H. A. Mason, To Homer through Pope (London, 1972), a polemical but serious study; Shewring's 'epilogue' to his translation of the Odyssey (pp. 299–330); Silk 1987, 46–54; A. Parry 1989, 39–49 (originally a review published in 1960); H. Lloyd-Jones, New York Review of Books 14 Feb. 1991 = Greek in a cold climate. (London, 1991), 1–17 (a review of Fagles' version with extensive comparisons).

Bibliographies

The fullest lists are published (always a few years later) by L'année philologique, an annual survey for all aspects of classical literature. The period from 1930–70 is documented by D. W. Packard and T. Meyers, A Bibliography of Homeric Scholarship (Malibu, 1974), which contains lists derived from L'année philologique and indexes of topics and passages discussed. For surveys including brief assessments see:

F. M. Combellack, 'Contemporary Homeric scholarship, sound or fury?' CW 49 (1955–6), 17–26, 29–44, 44–55.
J. P. Holoka, 'Homeric originality: a survey', CW 55 (1972–3), 257–93.
M. W. Edwards, 'Homer and oral tradition', Oral Tradition 1 (1986), 171–230, 3 (1988), 11–60.
M. E. Clark, 'Neoanalysis: a bibliographical review', CW 79 (1986), 379–94.
J. P. Holoka, 'Homer studies 1978–1983', CW 83 (1990), 393–461 and 84 (1990), 89–156.

There are also organized bibliographies in Latacz 1980 and 1991a, and many of the essays in Latacz 1991b are in effect bibliographical surveys (e.g. the contributions by Burkert on Oriental links, Graf on Religion and Mythology, Kullmann and Holoka on Neoanalysis). On orality and related debates see, besides Edwards above, J. M. Foley, The Theory of Oral Composition (Bloomington, 1988). For the speeches see Latacz, Grazer Beiträge 2 (1974) 395–422, Griffin 1986; for the similes, Moulton 1977, Edwards 1991, 24–41, and Rutherford 1992, 73–7. Stanley 1993 has a very full bibliography on most matters concerning the Iliad. For the Odyssey see Garvie 1994. Matters relating to narratology and critical methods are well-documented by de Jong, esp. 1987.

SELECT BIBLIOGRAPHY

General histories of Greek literature or of the epic genre are not included: the best short account of Homer in a work of that kind remains Albin Lesky's, in his *History of Greek Literature* (Eng. tr. by J. Willis and C. de Heer, London, 1966), 14–90.

ADKINS, A. W. H. 1960: *Merit and Responsibility: a Study in Greek Ethics* (Oxford).

ALLEN, T. W. 1924: *Homer: the Origins and the Transmission* (Oxford).

AUSTIN, N. 1975: *Archery at the Dark of the Moon: Poetic Problems in Homer's Odyssey* (Berkeley, Los Angeles, and London).

BANNERT, H. 1988: *Formen des Wiederholens bei Homer (Wiener Studien* Beiheft 13) (Vienna).

BOARDMAN, J. 1980: *The Greeks Overseas* (orig. 1964; revised and expanded edn.) (London).

BOWRA, C. M. 1930: *Tradition and Design in the Iliad* (Oxford).

—— 1961: *Heroic Poetry* (2nd edn.) (London).

BREMER, J. M., DE JONG, I., & KALFF, J. (edd.) 1987: *Homer: Beyond Oral Poetry* (Amsterdam).

BUFFIÈRE, F. 1956: *Les mythes d'Homère et la pensée grecque* (Paris).

BURKERT, W. 1987: 'The Making of Homer in the Sixth Century B.C.: Rhapsodes versus Stesichorus', *Papers on the Amasis Painter and his World* (J. Paul Getty Museum), 43–62.

—— 1992: *The Orientalizing Revolution. Near Eastern Influence on Greek Culture in the Early Archaic Age* (Cambridge Mass. and London).

CALHOUN, G. M. 1939:'Homer's Gods: Myth and Märchen', *AJP* 60, 1–28.

CARPENTER, RHYS 1946: *Folk-tale, Fiction and Saga in the Homeric Epics* (Berkeley and Los Angeles).

CLARK, M. E. 1986: 'Neoanalysis: a Bibliographical Review', *CW* 79, 379–94.

CLARKE, H. W. 1981: *Homer's Readers: a Historical Introduction to the Iliad and the Odyssey* (Newark, London, and Toronto).

COHEN, B. (ed.) 1995: *The Distaff Side: Representing the Female in Homer's Odyssey* (Oxford and N.Y.).

DE JONG, IRENE J. F. 1987: *Narrators and Focalizers: the Presentation of the Story of the Iliad* (Amsterdam).

—— 1988: 'Homeric Words and Speakers: an Addendum', *JHS* 108, 188–9.

—— 1991: 'Narratology and Oral Poetry: the Case of Homer', *Poetics Today* 12, 405–23.

DODDS, E. R. 1951: *The Greeks and the Irrational* (Berkeley and Los Angeles).

—— 1968: 'Homer and the Analysts', 'Homer and the Unitarians', 'Homer and Oral Poetry', in M. Platnauer (ed.), *Fifty Years and Twelve of Classical Scholarship* (revised version of *Fifty Years of Classical Scholarship*, 1956) (Oxford), 1–17, 31–5; repr. in Kirk 1964, 1–21.

DOVER, K. J. 1983: 'The Portrayal of Moral Evaluation in Greek Poetry', *JHS* 103, 35–48 = Dover, *Greek and the Greeks: Collected Papers I* (Oxford, 1987), 77–96.

EDWARDS, A. T. 1985: *Achilles in the Odyssey* (Beiträge zur Klass. Philol. 171) (Meisenheim).

EDWARDS, M. W. 1968: 'Some Stylistic Notes on *Iliad* xviii', *AJP* 89, 257–83.

—— 1987: *Homer, Poet of the Iliad* (Baltimore and London).

—— 1991: *The Iliad: a Commentary* vol. 5 (Books 17–20) (Cambridge).

EISENBERGER, H. 1973: *Studien zur Odyssee* (Wiesbaden).

EMLYN-JONES, C. 1984: 'The Reunion of Odysseus and Penelope', *G&R* 31, 1–18.

—— , HARDWICK, L. & PURKIS, J. (edd.) 1992: *Homer: Readings and Images* (London).

ERBSE, H. 1972: *Beiträge zum Verstandnis der Odyssee* (Berlin and N.Y.).

—— 1986: *Untersuchungen zur Funktion der Götter im homerischen Epos* (Berlin and N.Y.).

FENIK, B. 1968: *Typical Battle Scenes in the Iliad (Hermes* Einzelchriften 21) (Wiesbaden).

—— 1974: *Studies in the Odyssey (Hermes* Einzelschriften 30) (Wiesbaden).

—— (ed.) 1978: *Homer: Tradition and Invention* (Cincinnati Classical Studies n.s. 2) (Leiden).

FINLEY, M. I. 1954 (2nd edn. 1978): *The World of Odysseus* (New York; subsequently publ. in Penguin Classics, (Harmondsworth, 2nd edn. 1979).

—— , with CASKEY, J. L., KIRK, G. S., & PAGE, D. L. 1964: 'The Trojan War', *JHS* 84, 1–20.

FINNEGAN, R. 1977: *Oral poetry: its Nature, Significance and Social Context* (Cambridge).

FOXHALL, L., & DAVIES, J. K. (edd.) 1984: *The Trojan War, its Historicity and Context* (papers of the First Greenbank Colloquium, Liverpool) (Bristol).

FRÄNKEL, H. 1975: *Early Greek Poetry and Philosophy* (Eng. tr.) (Oxford).

GARVIE, A. F. 1994: *Homer, Odyssey 6–8*, with introd. and commentary (Cambridge).

GOLDHILL, S. 1991: *The Poet's Voice. Essays on Poetics and Greek Literature* (Cambridge).

GRAFTON, A. et al. 1987: see WOLF.

GRIFFIN, J. 1977: 'The Epic Cycle and the Uniqueness of Homer', *JHS* 97, 39–53.

—— 1980: *Homer on Life and Death* (Oxford).

—— 1986: 'Homeric Words and Speakers', *JHS* 106, 36–57.

—— 1987: *Homer: the Odyssey* (Landmarks in World Literature series) (Cambridge).

—— (ed.) 1995: *Homer, Iliad IX* (Oxford).

HAINSWORTH, J. B. 1969: *Homer (G&R* New Surveys 3; revised with additional bibl. 1979) (Oxford).

—— 1993: *The Iliad: a Commentary* vol. 3 (books 9–12) (Cambridge).

HALL, E. 1989: *Inventing the Barbarian: Greek Self-definition through Tragedy* (Oxford).

HANSEN, M. H. (ed.) 1993: *The Ancient City-State*. Acts of the Copenhagen Polis Centre, Vol. I (Copenhagen).

HATTO, A. T. (ed.) 1980: *Traditions of Heroic and Epic Poetry* i (London).

HERINGTON, J. 1985: *Poetry into Drama: Early Tragedy and the Greek Poetic Tradition* (Berkeley and L.A.).

HEUBECK, A., WEST, S. R. & HAINSWORTH, J. B. 1988: *A Commentary on Homer's Odyssey I* (Books 1–8) (Oxford).

HÖLSCHER, U. 1939: *Untersuchungen zur Form der Odyssee (Hermes* Einzelschr. 6) (Berlin).

JANKO, R. 1982: *Homer, Hesiod and the Hymns: Diachronic Development in Epic Diction* (Cambridge).

—— 1992: *The Iliad: a Commentary* vol. 4 (books 13–16) (Cambridge).

JEFFERY, L. H. 1961: *The Local Scripts of Archaic Greece*, 2nd edn. revised by A. Johnston, 1990 (Oxford).

JENSEN, MINNA SKAFTE 1980: *The Homeric Question and the Oral-Formulaic Theory* (Copenhagen).

JONES, PETER 1988: *Homer's Odyssey: a Companion to the English Translation of R. Lattimore* (Bristol).

—— 1991: *Homer: Odyssey 1 and 2* (Warminster).

KAKRIDIS, J. T. 1949: *Homeric Researches* (Lund).

—— 1971: *Homer Revisited* (Lund).

KIRK, G. S. 1962: *The Songs of Homer* (Cambridge) (There is an abridged version, *Homer and the Epic* (Cambridge, 1964)).

—— (ed.) 1964: *The Language and Background of Homer: Some Recent Studies and Controversies* (Cambridge).

—— 1970: *Myth: its Meaning and Function* (Berkeley and Los Angeles).

—— 1976: *Homer and the Oral Tradition* (Cambridge).

—— 1985: *The Iliad: a Commentary*, vol. 1 (Books 1–4) (Cambridge).

—— 1990: *The Iliad: a Commentary*, vol. 2 (Books 5–8) (Cambridge).

KRISCHER, T. 1971: *Formale Konventionen der homerischen Epik* (*Zetemata* 56) (Munich).

KULLMANN, W. 1960: *Die Quellen der Ilias* (*Hermes* Einzelschriften 14) (Wiesbaden).

—— 1985: 'Gods and Men in the *Iliad* and the *Odyssey*', *HSCP* 89, 1–23.

LAMBERTON, R., & KEANEY, J. (edd.) 1992: *Homer's Ancient Readers* (Princeton).

LATACZ, J. 1977: *Kampfparänese, Kampfdarstellung und Kampfwirklichkeit in der Ilias, bei Kallinos und Tyrtaios* (Zetemata 66) (Munich).

—— (ed.) 1979: *Homer, Tradition und Neuerung* (Wege der Forschung Bd. 463) (Darmstadt).

—— (ed.) 1991: *Zweihundert Jahre Homerforschung: Rückblick und Ausblick* (Stuttgart).

—— (ed.) 1991b: *Homer: Die Dichtung und ihre Deutung* (Wege der Forschung Bd. 634) (Darmstadt).

LESKY, A. 1961: *Göttliche und menschliche Motivation im homerischen Epos* (Heidelberg).

—— 1968: *Homeros, RE* Suppl. Bd. xi, 687–846 (also reprinted separately).

LLOYD-JONES, H. 1971 (2nd edn. 1983): *The Justice of Zeus* (Berkeley and L.A.).

LOHMANN, D. 1970: *Die Komposition der Reden in der Ilias* (Berlin).

LORD, A. B. 1960: *The Singer of Tales* (Cambridge, Mass.).

—— 1991: *Epic Singers and Oral Tradition* (Ithaca).

LYNN-GEORGE M. 1988: *Epos: Word, Narrative and the Iliad* (London).

MCAUSLAN, I. & WALCOT, P. (edd.) 1997 *Homer* (*G&R* Studies 4) (Oxford, forthcoming).

MACLEOD, C. W. 1982: *Homer, Iliad 24* (Cambridge).

—— 1983: 'Homer on Poetry and the Poetry of Homer' *Collected Essays*, 1–15 (Oxford).

MARTIN, R. P. 1989: *The Language of Heroes: Speech and Performance in the Iliad* (Ithaca and London).

MORRIS, I. 1986: 'The Use and Abuse of Homer', *ClAntiq.* 5, 81–138.

MOULTON, C. 1977: *Similes in the Homeric Poems* (*Hypomnemata* 49) (Göttingen).

MUELLER, MARTIN 1984: *The Iliad* (London).

MURNAGHAN, SHEILA 1987: *Disguise and Recognition in the Odyssey* (Princeton).

MURRAY, GILBERT 190   4th edn. 1934); *The Rise of the Greek Epic* (Oxford).

MURRAY, O. 1980 (2nd edn. 1993): *Early Greece* (London, Brighton, Glasgow).

NAGY, G. 1992: 'Homeric Questions', *TAPA* 122, 17–60.

—— 1996: *Poetry as Performance: Homer and Beyond* (Cambridge).

PAGE, D. 1955: *The Homeric Odyssey* (Oxford).

—— 1959: *History and the Homeric Iliad* (Berkeley and Los Angeles).

—— 1973: *Folk-tales in Homer's Odyssey* (Cambridge, Mass.).

PARRY, A. 1972: 'Language and Characterization in Homer', *HSCP* 76, 1–22 = A. Parry 1989, 310–25.

PARRY, ADAM 1989: *The Language of Achilles and other Papers*, ed. with foreword by H. Lloyd-Jones (Oxford).

PARRY, MILMAN 1971: *The Making of Homeric Verse: The Collected Papers of Milman Parry*, ed. Adam Parry (Oxford) (A. Parry's introduction, pp. ix–lxii, is reprinted in A. Parry 1989, 195–264).

PELLING, C. B. R. (ed.) 1990: *Characterization and Individuality in Greek Literature* (Oxford).

PFEIFFER, R. 1968: *History of Classical Scholarship from the Beginnings to the End of the Hellenistic Age* (Oxford).

RAAFLAUB, K. 1991: 'Homer und die Geschichte des 8. Jh. s.v. Christ' in Latacz 1991, 205–56.

—— 1993: 'Homer to Solon, The Rise of the Polis: the Written Sources', in *The Ancient City-State*, ed. M. H. Hansen (Acts of the Copenhagen Polis Centre vol. 1, Copenhagen), 41–105.

RADERMACHER, L. 1915: *Erzahlungen der Odyssee, SAWW* clxxviii (Vienna).

REDFIELD, JAMES M. 1975: *Nature and Culture in the Iliad: the Tragedy of Hector* (Chicago and London) (new edn. 1994, with additional ch. on the Gods).

REICHEL, M. 1994: *Fernbeziehungen in der Ilias* (ScriptOralia 62 A, Bd. 13) (Tübingen).

REINHARDT, K. 1948: 'Die Abenteuer des Odysseus' in Reinhardt, *Von Wege und Formen* (Godesburg), 52–162 = Reinhardt, *Tradition und Geist* (Göttingen, 1960), 47–124.

—— 1961: *Die Ilias and ihr Dichter* (Göttingen).

RICHARDSON, N. J. 1975: 'Homeric Professors in the Age of the Sophists', *PCPS* n.s. 21, 65–81.

—— 1980: 'Literary Criticism in the Exegetical Scholia to the *Iliad*' *CQ* n.s. 30, 265–87.

—— 1993: *The Iliad: a Commentary*, vol. 6 (books 21–24) (Cambridge).

ROSNER, J. A. 1976: 'The Speech of Phoenix: *Iliad* 9, 434–605', *Phoenix* 30, 314–27.

RUBINO, C. A. & SHELMERDINE, C. W. (edd.) 1983: *Approaches to Homer* (Austin, Texas).

RÜTER, K. 1969: *Odysseinterpretationen: Untersuchungen zum ersten Buch u. zur Phaiakis* (*Hypomnemata* 19) (Göttingen).

RUTHERFORD, R. B. 1982: 'Tragic Form and Feeling in the *Iliad*', *JHS* 102, 145–60.

—— 1985: 'At Home and Abroad: Aspects of the Structure of the *Odyssey*', *PCPS* n.s. 31, 133–50.

—— 1986: 'The Philosophy of the *Odyssey*', *JHS* 106, 145–62.

—— 1992: *Homer, Odyssey 19 and 20* (Cambridge).

—— 1991–3: 'From the *Iliad* to the *Odyssey*', *BICS* 38, 37–54 [actually published 1994].

SCHADEWALDT, W. 1943 (3rd ed. 1966): *Iliasstudien* (Leipzig).

—— 1944 (4th ed. 1965): *Von Homers Welt und Werk* (Stuttgart).

SCHEIN, S. L. 1984: *The Mortal Hero: an Introduction to Homer's Iliad* (Berkeley).

SEAFORD, RICHARD 1994: *Reciprocity and Ritual: Homer and Tragedy in the Developing City-State* (Oxford).

SEGAL, C. 1971: *The Theme of the Mutilation of the Corpse in the Iliad* (Mnemos. Suppl. 17) (Leiden).

—— 1995: *Singers, Heroes and Gods in the Odyssey* (Ithaca and London).

SILK, M. S. 1987: *Homer: the Iliad* (Landmarks in World Literature series) (Cambridge).

SLATKIN, L. M. 1991: *The Power of Thetis. Allusion and Interpretation in the Iliad* (Berkeley and Los Angeles).

SNELL, B. 1953: *The Discovery of the Mind: the Greek Origins of European Thought* (Oxford).

SOURVINOU-INWOOD, C. 1995: '*Reading' Greek Death to the end of the Classical Period* (Oxford).

STANFORD, W. B. 1963: *The Ulysses Theme* (2nd edn.) (Oxford).

—— & LUCE, J. V. 1974: *The Quest for Ulysses* (London).

STANLEY, K. 1993: *The Shield of Homer: Narrative Structure in the Iliad* (Princeton).

STEWART, DOUGLAS J. 1976: *The Disguised Guest: Rank, Role and Identity in the Odyssey* (Lewisberg).

TAPLIN, O. 1990: 'Agamemnon's Role in the *Iliad*' in Pelling 1990, 60–92.

—— 1992: *Homeric Soundings: the Shaping of the Iliad* (Oxford).

TAYLOR, CHARLES H., JR. (ed.) 1963: *Essays on the Odyssey: Selected Modern Criticism* (Bloomington and London).

THALMANN, W. G. 1984: *Conventions of Form and Thought in Early Greek Epic Poetry* (Baltimore).

THORNTON, A. 1970: *People and Themes in Homer's Odyssey* (London).

—— 1984: *Homer's Iliad: its Composition and the Motif of Supplication* (*Hypomnemata* 81) (Göttingen).

TSAGARAKIS, O. 1982: *Form and Content in Homer* (*Hermes* Einzelschr. 46) (Wiesbaden).

VAN WEES, H. 1992: *Status-Warriors. War, Violence and Society in Homer and History* (Amsterdam).

VERMEULE, E. 1979: *Aspects of Death in Early Greek Art and Poetry* (Berkeley and Los Angeles).

VIDAL-NAQUET, P. 1970: 'Valeurs religieuses et mythiques de la terre et du sacrifice dans l'Odyssée', *Annales ESC* 25, 1278–97 (revised Eng. tr. in R. Gordon (ed.) *Myth, religion and society* (Cambridge, 1981), 80–94).

WACE, A. J. B. & STUBBINGS, F. H. (edd.) 1962: *A Companion to Homer* (London).

WADE-GERY, H. T. 1952: *The Poet of the Iliad* (Cambridge).

WENDER, DOROTHEA 1978: *The Last Scenes of the Odyssey* (Mnemos. Suppl. 52) (Leiden).

WEST, M. L. 1988: 'The Rise of the Greek Epic', *JHS* 108, 151–72.

WEST, S. 1988: refers to her contributions to Heubeck, West & Hainsworth 1988.

—— 1989: 'Laertes Revisited', *PCPS* n.s. 35, 113–43.

WHITMAN, C. 1958: *Homer and the Heroic Tradition* (Cambridge, Mass.).

WILLCOCK, M. M. 1976: *A companion to the Iliad* (Chicago and London).

WINKLER, J. J. 1990: *The Constraints of Desire: the Anthropology of Sex and Gender in Ancient Greece* (London and N.Y.).

WOLF, F. A. 1985 (1795): *Prolegomena to Homer*, ed. and tr. A. Grafton, G. W. Most, and J. E. G. Zetzel (Princeton, N.J.).

WOODHOUSE, W. J. 1930: *The Composition of Homer's Odyssey* (Oxford).

WRIGHT, JOHN (ed.) 1978: *Essays on the Iliad: Selected Modern Criticism* (Bloomington and London).

ZANKER, G. 1974: *The Heart of Achilles: Characterization and Personal Ethics in the Iliad* (Ann Arbor, Michigan).

ABOUT THE AUTHOR

Dr Rutherford was born in Edinburgh in 1956, and educated at Robert Gordon's College, Aberdeen, and at Worcester College, Oxford. Since 1982 he has been Tutor in Greek and Latin Literature at Christ Church, Oxford. Besides his work on Homer, he is the author of *The Meditations of Marcus Aurelius: a Study* (Oxford, 1989), and of *The Art of Plato: Ten Essays in Platonic Interpretation* (London, 1995). He has also written various articles on both Greek and Latin authors.

INDEX

This index is deliberately selective; it is intended mainly to help readers find the principal discussion of a given topic.